Be The Better Person

Be The Better Person

The secret to your
happy-peaceful-content life
in this greedy-confused-unloving world is

The Golden Rule

By: Mary Miner & GOD

authorHOUSE®

AuthorHouse™
1663 Liberty Drive
Bloomington, IN 47403
www.authorhouse.com
Phone: 1-800-839-8640

First published by AuthorHouse   10/25/2011

ISBN: 978-1-4634-4552-2 (sc)
ISBN: 978-1-4634-4551-5 (ebk)

Library of Congress Control Number: 2011913604

Printed in the United States of America

Any people depicted in stock imagery provided by Thinkstock are models, and such images are being used for illustrative purposes only.
Certain stock imagery © Thinkstock.

This book is printed on acid-free paper.

Contents

GREETING

Hi There!

My name is Mary Miner. I was guided, pushed and supported, spiritually and financially by GOD to write this golden book just as many other authors have been guided to write books to help make OUR world a better place. That sounds trite I know but we really need to keep trying to make our world a better place; don't you agree? If you don't agree then maybe this golden book is not for you. Please put it back on the shelf and leave it for someone who does agree.

I don't know why I was chosen to write this golden book and share with you THE SECRETS TO YOUR HAPPY-PEACEFUL-CONTENT LIFE IN THIS GREEDY-CONFUSED-UNLOVING WORLD. I guess GOD needed a hand and I am so fortunate to be there for HIM just as HE has been there for me. That may sound arrogant but you will see what I mean as you read through Our golden book.

My husband, he was chosen too. He also gets credit. Because of him I was able to discern these "secrets". However, I must mention he didn't have to "find himself" or search for happiness as much as I did because he is innately happy. His glass is not half full or half empty. His glass is constantly over flowing. These secrets to him are common sense. "Being happy is not rocket science," my retired Marine of twenty years in the Marine Corps would say. Having him in my life has helped me realize that life IS and can be fun.

Nonetheless, I am so excited to share, enhance and balance these secrets with you. Most notably, GOD gets most of the credit because HE is my driving force so I can write this golden book. With that said; this brings me to a very important proverb.

"Credit is due where credit is deserved," Peggy Fuller, my first mother in law

Those that come up with good ideas, great thoughts or creative actions should get the deserved credit. Wouldn't you agree that people crave to be recognized for their talents but often times are not? Do you know for most people it is easier to criticize than to compliment? To Us (GOD and me), that is sad. Isn't it true that so few of us actually take the time to compliment others? More of this will be discussed in Chapter 7, Pay It Forward.

Throughout this golden book I am going to share how I became The Better Person. It took half my life to seek this truth and happiness and now GOD has asked me to share how you too can become The Better Person and find the inner happiness you might be longing. Hopefully this golden book and other material that I mention will help you on your own personal journey of becoming The Better

Person. See the Appendix, for a list of great influential reading.

I must thank you for taking the time to read this golden book. I know GOD and I can help as long as you truly try to understand and believe Our concepts and philosophies. Most important though is you have to first want to be The Better Person. You have to want to make a difference in yourself and those around you. Our concepts, philosophy and techniques are really quite simple but it will take a conscious effort on your part. So, if you decide you want to be The Better Person; then please keep reading. Otherwise, if being The Better Person is not important to you, please put this golden book back on the shelf until you are ready to work on having a better life.

The payoff for your efforts are not only rewarding; it's fun and great for everyone. Once you practice these golden skills, you will see how your life will positively change. You will also have a better grasp of how you can embrace the difficulties in your life, accepting each and every event as part of your journey. You will be able to solve problems with smart solutions, and know when to let go and let GOD.

When you apply these golden skills, you will love yourself more than you do right now. Wow, what a thought!

You will not only wake up with a smile almost every morning (can't say every morning because no one but GOD and Jesus can wake up every morning with a smile), but you will feel so different inside; almost like you are a glowing light. You will have some of those bad days but much less often and you will know what to do when you do have them. However, the hardest part is to get started and continue to consistently work on being The Better Person. This is a life time journey; not a quick fix.

Just to let you know, I capitalize GOD, "Our", "Us" and "We" throughout this golden book because GOD is my higher power and this is my way of showing HIM respect. I say HE and HIM because HE is my FATHER. I only mentioned that for those of you who have a hard time discerning if GOD is a male or female. What does it matter anyway?

HE says that I need to share these golden techniques with those who will listen. It makes perfect sense. I know perfect is a very strong word, too strong for me but just right for GOD. Thus, Our mission is to get everyone to WANT to be The Better Person because it is fun and feels so good. Not only that, if I can share with you and consistently practice what HE has taught me, that shows that I have mastered these golden skills myself and that is my goal.

Ironically it is usually those who read books like this one that are already kind, considerate and sincere givers. I bet you are one of the few that continuously share your time, love and are a very caring human being. If you are anything like me, you picked up this golden book because sometimes it is hard to <u>always</u> be The Better Person and you are looking for an answer to your current situation. Or you might be having a bad or difficult day. A book like this is a great pick me up book; somewhat of an incentive to get you back on track. It's a good book to keep so that you can refer back to it when you are having another one of those days.

I know when I am having a bad day, I head to the library or bookstore to check out a book or audio that will bring back my loving spirit. I have Mary days where I hide behind a really good inspirational book; just like this one. Those are the days when I am "just not right", as they say in the South. Either I am hurt, angry, sad, jealous or just plain moody. Do you have days like that? Dah! Of course you do. This is when I need my self-help book fix. It works for a week or two until I am down again. That actually went on and off for about 30 years. I even got to the point where I was taking an anti-depressant. I no longer need it because I have finally found most of the answers to a happier, peaceful, content life. Thank you GOD! Hopefully, with the help of this golden book; it won't take you as long. For those of you who are fighting depression, if you practice what We are teaching in this golden book; you probably won't have to take a pill to make you feel better. If We can bring more happiness and peace to your life, this golden book would be worth all Our efforts. Isn't that what you strive for; is a happier, peaceful and content life?

I just want to mention; it is those that don't read self help books that need to know about this golden book and Our way of thinking. I will give you credit too when you become The Better Person. Thus, WE is capitalized because it will take millions, including yourself and GOD to make this world a better place. Our is capitalized because as I mentioned earlier GOD is telling me to write this. It is HIS idea just my writings. WE will have to teach others to WANT to be The Better Person and show them the benefits of doing so. That's why this golden book must be a success; a #1 National Best Seller. For those that don't normally read books like these, will pick this golden book up because everyone is talking about it.

Thus, if you would tell others and demonstrate Our concepts and philosophies; they too will most likely follow your actions because they will see that you are a much happier, peaceful and content person. Hopefully, they will want what you are experiencing. While you read this golden book, we will want you to share your ideas on bethebetterperson.org. You will get recognized when you give examples of how you were The Better Person on any given day.

Just think, if these golden thoughts could spreads across and throughout the world, what a difference WE could make. Do you remember the Coca-Cola commercial "I'd Like to Teach the World to Sing in Perfect Harmony"? It depicted millions of people holding hands in harmony across the globe. As I was growing up, I always wondered why that commercial was significant to me. Now, I know why. It is all GOD'S plan for me.

However, I cannot do it without you. I need your help to get to the greedy corrupted ones. Mean people are the ones We really want to reach. They know who they are? Are you one of them?

So if you like Our ideas, please tell your friends how enlightening this golden book is, so they get curious and borrow or buy the golden book so I can turn around with the money I make and get this message out to the world so we could live in a better place with better people. I know it sounds like a dream but Martin Luther King Jr., he had a dream and for the most part, it came true. If we can get "the selfish, mean people" to pick up this golden book then hopefully they too will understand and enjoy the rewards of being The Better Person. WE can make a change together. This is not just a book, it is the beginning of a campaign, a legacy. Wow, what a challenge. Up for it? I hope so.

Me, I need constant guidance. I read self help books all the time. I used to hide them when I checked them out at the library or said they were for a friend when I bought them at the bookstore. Just recently I became proud that I read all those "self-help" books because they created who I am today. It took me a long time to realize that I should be proud that I seek wisdom from others and that I am trying to better myself every day.

You can read this golden book actively or passively. It's just a choice of what you want to get out of it. I will provide exercises that will help you remember how you did things in the past, how you presently go about your day and how you could be doing them Our way. Hopefully this golden book is easy reading because I cannot tolerate books that I have to read the sentence over three or four times before I understand what it said.

> Tangent: This reminds me of watching a movie and everyone in the room goes, "what did he/ she say"? Think about it, if more than one person says, what did he/she say, then many others watching the same movie didn't hear it either. Especially when you rewind the program and you still can't hear what they are saying. What I wonder is, when directors are making a movie or show and want it to be a success, then why in the world do they continue to create scenes where you cannot hear or understand everything that is being said. One of my pet peeves as you might have noticed. Just thought I would mention that just in case a director of a movie is reading this. But isn't it true? I do go off on tangents every once; they will be written in this format.

Again, you will only want to read something over because it made you think, not because you had a hard time understanding the point. Also I am writing this golden book over a period of a year and during that year I too am challenged daily and have to consistently work on being The Better Person. Thus, these are some of my personal experiences and my perceptions. I won't mention names. I do not want to hurt anyone. I am writing so hopefully you can learn from my mistakes and grow with love. I struggle daily at doing what GOD wants me to do. Sure it's not easy but the reward is so peaceful and calming.

One other thing before we get started, this golden book is not about me getting rich and making money. This golden book is about helping and changing OUR world. To make it a better place on a daily basis. I live a humble life. Just like you, I want to have a beautiful home. However, you won't see me carrying a $100 purse or suited in name brand clothing or a statue or fountain in my yard, except for a bird bath or two. I would rather take that money and give it to someone who I could help have a better life. We, my Marine and I, constantly give and will continue to give and help others because that is what brings us more happiness. If you do the same and follow the concepts and philosophies of this golden book, you too can experience a more happy peaceful, content life. I am just a simple person with GOD'S powerful message on a mission to "Be The Better Person".

One last note before revealing the secrets to your happy, peaceful and content life; I used the words always, everything, every, each time, etc throughout this golden book. It's funny because as I was writing I had second thoughts on using those difinitive words so I changed them. Then my INNER VOICE told me to not save what I changed because HE <u>always</u> wants us to try <u>every</u> time. See, I am not the only one writing this golden book. ☺. We know that it is not always easy to be The

Better Person but if you always try then you will learn faster. In exchange you will obtain a happier, peaceful and more content life. That is your goal, isn't it? Well, if this is not your goal, please give this golden book to someone else or put it back on the shelf.

As I proof-read and proof-read this golden book, I noticed more grammatical errors. Please excuse the ones I missed and just be attentive to the message. I am not blessed with the talent of an editor and GOD just told me not to be worried about it because someone will volunteer to edit Our book. So if you are that someone, please contact me at alwaysbethebetterperson@yahoo.com. We need to get this message out.

To Summarize:

- GOD is my force in writing this golden book.
- Put this golden book back and/or recycle it if you don't want to be The Better Person.
- Credit goes where credit is deserved.
- After reading this golden book, if you practice Our philosophy, you will love yourself and YOUR life more than you do today.
- This is a great pick me up book, keep it on the shelf for those bad days.
- Please share this golden book with those that you know are greedy, mean and really need a positive change in their life.
- Help me get on a talk show. Please checkout my website and join this campaign and be part of a legacy.

INTRODUCTION

Listen to your INNER VOICE

Let's start with, some of you don't believe in GOD or any sort of Higher Power. That is your prerogative. It is not for me to judge. If you can go through life all by yourself and find true happiness, peace and be kind to everyone without any help from a Higher Power, then my hat goes off to you.

For those of you who do believe in GOD or a Higher Power then you probably also believe or are working on believing that everything happens for a reason and everyday is just exactly the way it is supposed to be. You are probably also smart enough to realize that you have a good amount of control on how and when you want things to happen, right?

In my case I could have done something unproductive today, like play mindless spider solitary or worked in my garden. However I know I have a job to do for GOD because I listened to my INNER VOICE. HE has provided me with more than necessary thus I want to serve HIM the best I can. So obviously we do have the opportunity to make our own choices.

You also probably know that those choices actually create who you are. To take it one step further, your choices can also produce your destiny. My destiny is to spread as much love on this earth as I possibly can. It is a huge project for me because I often fight being grumpy with a loving spirit. Sounds like an oxymoron, I know. GOD knows this about me as well; yet HE also knows that I have the capability to get HIS message to you.

Nonetheless, once you truly believe everything in your life happens for a reason and it is exactly the way it is supposed to be with you in control; your life will be much easier to live and you won't question what I just said.

So, with learning to see my truth for what it is, I continue on my mission to write a book that GOD wanted you to read. I would like to share with you how I know that GOD wants me to do this.

I was living in Orlando and wasn't happy. I wrote in my journal almost daily and I was approaching 50 and I needed to make a change. The old adage "I wasn't getting any younger" was my mantra. Now was the time to move so that I could rebuild my sales business before I got any older. Cold calling in 90 degree weather is hard on the body. I also knew if I stayed I would always say to myself; I should have left.

Moreover though, there was this FORCE, that guided me everyday through this adventurous transition. Things happened so fast. We found the most beautiful home in the country, one neighbor with 500 acres of cows. We knew this was our dream home. The love of my life at the time and my husband now, who I call my Marine throughout this golden book, loved our new home in SC that he just quit his high paying job in Orlando. He had TOTAL FAITH that everything would be ok. People thought we were crazy. I thought he was out of his mind. Nope, he just had TOTAL FAITH. How can we just move to another state without a job? How will we survive? My Daddy would say, "Mary, there are times you just have to be satisfied with where you are at, especially when you have such good jobs."

Our excitement, my mate's TOTAL FAITH and GOD would help us survive. My Marine was also on a mission. He had a dream to own a concession trailer and cook for a living. We used our retirement and took a risk. GOD told me not to. I didn't listen. Well, we bought a concession trailer, worked three festivals and he worked at it daily for a couple of months and we lost over $20,000. I guess that was my lesson for not listening to HIM.

It got tough. We lost weight eating not much of anything but concession left-overs. We were broke. No cable, no internet, no air conditioning, slept in the cold, no extras. But we didn't care because we were in a beautiful home and had each other. Blessed, my gas was paid for with my job. We had enough money to barely pay our bills. I cried often, got scared and cried out to GOD.

It was October 2008 when GOD told me everything will be ok and that HE wouldn't take the beautiful home we just bought or our vehicles. HE continuously assured us that even though the economy was falling HE would provide. HE also told me to have TOTAL FAITH and to dream big even when my sales were not going well. I was crying on a daily basis because I was living in fear but kept TOTAL FAITH. I wrote in my journal to help me get through these tough times. On October 2, 2008, HE told me to "Flip forward about 10 empty pages and write. SOMETHING BIG IS COMING MY WAY. TO DREAM BIG!

I stopped crying and one day while I was lying in bed thinking about how I can decorate our home. "DREAM BIG" GOD told me. "DREAM BIG". This was hard for me to do because I am a simple person and I give more than I get. I love to create or make things but I wasn't the shopping type to just go out and buy expensive stuff.

For months my INNER VOICE kept saying, "SOMETHING BIG IS COMING." "KEEP WORKING AS HARD AS YOU ARE." "DREAM BIG." "KEEP DOING EVERYTHING WITH LOVE." TURN THE PAGE ABOUT FIVE TO TEN PAGES AND WRITE THIS AGAIN AND TURN THE PAGES AND WRITE IT AGAIN. I did. I would show these "ADVISED" entrees to my Marine and he wanted to believe too. At that point we were so astounded that we didn't have a choice but to believe. Everything was happening just the way HE planned for me. Above and below are the actual journal entries. Of course I deleted my private entries.

4

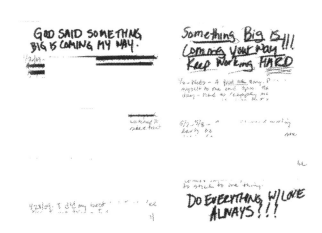

SOMETHING BIG did come our way and as I write everyday is better and better. Funny how in the worst economy since The Great Depression; we both got incredible jobs. We are not only making money helping Veterans but we have time. I no longer have to get up a 5am, work till 9pm. We are fat again, not really but not going to bed hungry. We bought a Christmas tree before Thanksgiving because we hadn't had one for two years. We are living large, not as large as an executive because we are simple people but we are once again enjoying our life almost stress free. The only stress we have is the stress we create.

I thank GOD on an hourly basis for my wonderful Marine, my high paying job, my beautiful very low maintenance country home, my cool dependable blue car, my soon to be flourishing garden, my yard that if I didn't do a thing, it would be beautiful just the way it is, the best dog in the whole wide world, my talking cat, my beauty, my concerned and generous family, my loving friends, and most important my peace of mind.

To Summarize:

- Everything happens for a reason. Once you believe this your life will get easier for you.
- My story of why We are writing this golden book
- If you listen to your INNER VOICE, there is a mission for you as well
- Maybe you are supposed to help Us with this campaign. If so, please go to my www. bethebetterperson.org.
- Others talk to GOD, you can too.
- Might think I am crazy; frankly I don't care if you think that because if this is what it takes for me and you to be The Better Person then I want to be crazy, don't you?
- If you don't agree with this golden book, please put it back on the shelf or recycle it.
- Either way, thank-you for taking a look at it.

CHAPTER 1

THE GOLDEN RULE
Who Is The Better Person?

You are! If you choose to be. If you see the truth for what it is, you can look at every situation, every day and be The Better Person if you want to be. All you need to do is ALWAYS practice:

THE GOLDEN RULE

Do unto others
as you would want them
to do unto you.

Or simplified

Treat others
as you would like to be treated

It is that simple. Not! It is not simple at all or we would all be doing it, right?

It actually takes practice, processing, practice, more processing, and sometimes even more processing to develop this golden skill.

Better yet, when you can teach it and practice what you preach every waking hour, you will have mastered it. I am not there yet. However it is just our choice, isn't it?

From the time we get up in the morning until we lay our head down. It's just a choice of how kind, considerate and sincere we want to be. For some, this manner is innate; it's natural for you. However, for most of us, sad to say, it will take a conscious effort to <u>ALWAYS </u>be <u>c</u>onsistently <u>k</u>ind, <u>c</u>onsiderate and <u>s</u>incere. (CKCS). I will sometimes use these acronyms throughout this golden book. These are the logical fundamental characteristics that We want you to work on. There are more but We want to keep it simple. Consistently is the challenge and should be our goal to be The Better Person. Sure most of us are KCS but very few are CKCS, agree?

You would think that those who believe in GOD and attend church regularly would diligently practice THE GOLDEN RULE because THIS RULE is present in almost every religion. Go to: www.unification.net/ws/theme015. htm to see how many religions are supposed to live by THE GOLDEN RULE.

For the most part, we can say that many of us try to follow THE GOLDEN RULE. But you would be surprised at how many people, even those that go to church, are not consistently kind, considerate and sincere. Again, many do but many many more don't. Stop for a second, being true to yourself, especially if you seek GOD, ask yourself, are you CKCS and do you practice THE GOLDEN RULE daily?

Let me share a story with you. I am a mortgage loan officer. I visit many home owners in their personal residence to help them refinance their loans. One afternoon, I was welcomed into a house with a warm greeting from the husband but his wife was unsure of me and thought I was selling a scam. To be understood; most people are skeptical about our product and services at first. I quickly noticed many ornate crucifixes and classical pictures of Jesus and other church decor. As I normally am, I was kind, considerate and sincere. My presentation was not pushy and I truly wanted to help this Veteran save money. If I could not have saved them money then I would have thanked them for their time and left. However this Veteran was going to save about $10,000 in just eight years. Well, the husband saw the savings and was very impressed with what I came to offer but she didn't like our loan or me and started to raise her voice. She unnecessarily treated me unkindly. I stopped her with gentle words and told her I truly want the best for her and her husband. As I tried to calm her, I looked around and sincerely complimented her on her beautiful church decor. She ignored my compliments. I told her I love GOD with all my heart and wasn't there to hurt them. She continued to be rude to me. Then she announced that I was wasting her time because she had to go to church. Her tone was harsh and unnecessarily mean. Wow, I said to myself peacefully, I don't think she quite understands the message GOD is trying to send to people through going to church. She definitely was not practicing THE GOLDEN RULE but yet she goes to church three times a week. Hmmm. There is definitely something wrong with this picture? I really wonder what she gets out of going to church. She obviously doesn't trust sales people and that's fine but I gave her no reason whatsoever to be unkind to

For example: With my share and tell, I am telling about my third grade and I am answering the question who was my favorite teacher. **1.** That was Mrs. Watanabe. I must have been eight. **2.** I remember there were four portables and we were in the first one next to the stairs at Maunawili Elementary in Hawaii. I think they were air conditioned. We didn't have AC in the other classrooms. **3.** I was with my classmates. **4 & 5.** I was passing out papers in my pretty blue dress. **6.** I kissed Ronnie S's paper before I gave it to him. He didn't see. If he only knew. I had a crush on him. Mrs. Watanabe was so nice to me. She made me feel special. She knew the kids didn't like me and I had problems at home and she let me stay in the class room and correct papers after school. **7.** To this day, I am a still a very studious romantic woman and some-what of a loner.

Let's get started on you. Also, go ahead share it on our website as well if you would like to.

What is your very first memory?

Now, let's go to your first years of school. It might be daycare, preschool or elementary. Remember to ask the above seven questions with almost every main question. Some questions don't call for them.

Your first experience with school

1. **Who got you up in the morning?**
2. **Breakfast, what did you eat?**
3. **Who cooked it for you?**
4. **How did you get to school?**
5. **What were your school experiences?**

6. Did the teacher like you?
7. What did she teach you?
8. Who were your favorite teachers?
9. Ever think to call them, write them, find them on Facebook?
10. Who were your friends?
11. Were they nice to you, mean, jealous?
12. What about recess, did you have friends to hang out with?
13. What did you do for lunch?
14. Who was home for you when you got home?
15. Who helped you with your homework?
16. What activities did you have for after school?
17. Who made sure you brushed your teeth and took a bath?
18. Who cooked dinner?
19. Who cleaned up?
20. Who took the time to read you bed time stories?
21. Who tucked you in at night?
22. What did you learn from the questions above?

Repeat the above with third, fourth and fifth grade.

23. Ok, now what about the fourth, fifth, and sixth; what values stuck that you are now teaching your own children or taught them as they were growing up?
24. Write teenage values here please
25. How were you awakened in the morning?
26. Breakfast, what did you eat?
27. Who made it for you?

28. How did you get to school?
29. What were your school experiences?
30. Did the teacher like you?
31. What did she teach you?
32. Who were your favorite teachers?
33. Who were your friends?
34. Were they nice to you, mean, jealous?
35. What about between classes, did you have friends to hang out with?
36. What did you eat for lunch?
37. Who was home for you when you got home?
38. Who reminded you to do your homework, made sure you brushed your teeth and made sure you took a shower? Yes, I am sure someone had to remind you.
39. What activities did you have for after school?
40. Who cooked dinner?
41. Who cleaned up?
    Now go back to Middle School and High School
42. How were you awaken in the morning?
43. Breakfast, what did you eat?
44. Who made it for you?
45. How did you get to school
46. What were you school experiences?
47. Did the teacher like you? Why or why not?
48. What did they teach you?
49. Who were your favorite teachers?
50. Who were your friends?
51. Were they nice to you, mean, jealous?
52. What about between periods, did you have friends to hang out with?
53. Who was home for you when you got home?

54. **Who made you do your homework, made sure you brushed your teeth and showered?**
55. **What activities did you have for after school?**
56. **Who cooked dinner?**
57. **What was your favorite meal?**
58. **Who cleaned up?**
59. **Who did you say good night?**
60. **Did you practice THE GOLDEN RULE?**
Go ahead, share and tell about every year after.

There are three reasons for this long exercise. One, it's fun and we rarely ever share with others our past life in detail because there are not too many people that care or want to listen. If you don't have a true friend, you actually have to pay a person to listen to who you were as a child and what you did. I want you to share with me on my website your life stories. Details friend, details.

The second reason is to see if you have ever thanked the people that raised you. We will discuss this in detail in Chapter 3.

The third reason is to see if you and your family practiced THE GOLDEN RULE. Did you? My goal here is to have you recognize that you are probably not applying THE GOLDEN RULE as much as you should be, with your family, or friends, co-workers and especially those customer services representatives you deal with when you want to use or get rid of their products.

If you weren't taught or remember anything good because you had such a horrible childhood, what have you taught yourself? You do have a bigger challenge because you would have to teach yourself and rely on yourself. Do your values include THE GOLDEN RULE?

I was taught to say thank you more than please. I was taught to not only share but I was taught to do the right thing and punished when I didn't; thank-you Mom and Dad. I was not taught THE GOLDEN RULE outright. However, my oldest sister demonstrated IT to me when I became a teenage; she always looked out for me and she generously gave me things that she wanted for herself. In fact the opposite was true in my younger years. I didn't even know what respect was because in my house; there was no respect for anyone. Constant yelling and fighting is what I remember. My Mom was mentally ill and my Dad generously supported our family. My family didn't know how to deal with my Mom's illness. We did the best the best we could. My parents were taught that way and so were we. We knew how to be seen and not heard. We knew how to sit at a dinner table with no elbows on the table and keep a really clean house. Most nobly, we did learn how important it was to give and not expect anything in return. I am not angry with my parents for the way I was brought up, they just DID NOT NOW HOW to raise kids, because they were never taught how to love, honor and respect each other in their families. I wouldn't change anything because I wouldn't be the beautiful person I am today.

I learned about THE GOLDEN RULE from reading my self-help books from ages 20-40. The ones that changed my life were: *Dance with Anger* by Harriet Lerner; *In the Meantime* by Iyanla Vanzant; and *Conversations with GOD, Book 1, by* Neale Walsch. However, THE GOLDEN RULE didn't sink into my heart until my teenage son and I were having a yelling match. That was the biggest, brightest light bulb that ever went off. My son was doing something teenagers do and I was yelling at him, "why don't you respect me, stop yelling at me." He bellowed back, "why don't you respect me! You need to stop yelling at me." "Think about it Mom, you taught us THE GOLDEN RULE and you want me to be The Better Person but you need to practice what you preach".

WOW! He was right! My life changed from that day on. Sure I yelled at some people after that, but I was either very careful or apologized for my out burst. I was raised to yell. Not only did my parents yell in anger, my father was slightly deaf and thus we came from a very loud home. I learned and changed my way of expressing myself. It took a while before I stopped yelling but if I started to yell; I stopped myself and gave myself a time out and walked away. At first I stomped away, slamming doors, and moving things loudly as I walked. Now I walk away with a more quiet attitude and I rarely get livid like I did in the past. Every once in a while I still have a short quick outburst of temporary anger. Skillfully, I catch myself and excuse myself from the situation. Before I walk away, I breathe gently, calmly and composed and I say, "that upset me and I need a moment please; I will be back to discuss it".

Now, I yell on paper, not at the person. I normally don't send it because I realize that isn't practicing THE GOLDEN RULE and I wouldn't be any better of a person if I did. When I am angry, I stop and go silent and think first before I speak. Sometimes I have to ask for a time out and just walk away, write and come back to the situation. However, since I am trying to master THE GOLDEN RULE, I don't get angry that often. I am human and I will continue to get frustrated and angry but I will control my action because I am striving daily to be The Better Person.

Let me ask you this, do you even like THE GOLDEN RULE? If not, please put this back on the self and pick it up when you want peace in your life and are tired of a hectic dramatic life. You might not be ready for a book like this; and that is ok. I bought, borrowed many books that I wasn't ready for. Many times, months or sometimes years would pass and I would pick up the same book and at that time I would understand and enjoy what the author was trying to convey. So, don't be too concerned because when you are ready the teacher will come.

For those of you who do believe in THE GOLDEN RULE, do you always treat all people the way you want to be treated? Of course you don't. You would all be saints if you did. It is not likely that you treat others the way you want to be treated **all** the time. GOD too doesn't expect it **all** the time; HE just wants you to try to do IT **all** the time.

So what are some things we can do daily, hourly and by the minute that is considered practicing THE GOLDEN RULE. I mentioned earlier that being consistently kind, considerate and sincere are the fundamentals of THE GOLDEN RULE but I want to take it to even a higher level; which brings me to a sub-chapter because it goes hand in hand with THE GOLDEN RULE.

If You Do Everything with Love You Cannot Fail

Let me explain each word of this proverb.

If: If means it is your choice to do so.

You: that's you, dah

Do: Your action, your tone of voice, your reaction.

Everything: every move you make, every sound you make or any move or sound you don't make.

With: a connecting word

LOVE: the most important word, follow THE GOLDEN RULE; if you like being treated like that, they will too

You: that's you again ☺. See you are in control

Cannot: won't happen

Fail: be wrong; opposite of succeed; your own connotation

In other words, if you carry out all your daily tasks and other life situations with love; doing your best every day to handle each situation with sincere kindness, consideration to all involved; you will experience a feeling of accomplishment even if the outcome didn't work out the way you expected it to.

If you also learn to be consistently kind, considerate and sincere to even your adversaries, you will achieve a happier, more peaceful, content life because you will know in your heart that you did your absolute best with love and therefore you won't feel like you should have handled the situation differently than you did. That is a great feeling. You have exhausted all means in a loving manner. When you know that you did the right thing, you feel better than you do if you did the wrong thing, don't you? I also am sure you understand what I mean because we have all said something we wished we hadn't many of times.

However, once you practice doing everything with love on a daily basis, you will not only understand what We are trying to convey but more importantly, you will feel great and will want to share this feeling with your family and friends. Feeling good is what you are trying to accomplish, isn't it? If not please put this golden book on back on the shelf or give it away; because it will eventually find the person who is ready to experience a more happy, peaceful and content life.

Let me explain. It really is common sense but many of you have not figured it out yet. Let Us help so you don't have to do this on your own.

Let's say you didn't get the promotion you wanted or you had to give up your son because you ex-husband was making your life and your son's life miserable or you have to leave your wife because she is a mean drunk or your husband had an affair or a co-worker is talking stink about you so they can look better than you or something as simple as you were over charged on a bill, or someone cut in front of you in the line at the store. Most of these situations occur all the time, don't they? Just curious, what was your last frustrating situation in the past week, or month that made you angry? Tell me about it on my website.

It sucked to be you, didn't it? Just a little humor; I hope you laughed. I like that saying. My son used to tell me that. It often times lightens the situation when you say it.

How you feel will most likely come impulsively. Of course, you have every right to feel the way you do. Although some of us make the situation worse with unnecessary emotions which can be very time consuming, right? More on this will be discussed in Chapter 5.

Either way, you know you are in control of how you handle any given situation. We want you to handle even your toughest, most tragic situations with love. We want you to learn that as long as you know you did your absolute best with love you will have a more peaceful mindset on a daily basis. When you do apply THE GOLDEN RULE, to all those involved including yourself, in every situation then you cannot possibly be or feel like a looser.

You will probably feel temporarily defeated, hurt, or some other emotion but if you know in your heart that you exhausted all means with love and realize there is not any more you can do. You will at that time be able to let go faster. It will get easier for you to get on with your day. Isn't that a nice thought? The sooner you realize that when you present yourself with humble pride and conviction but with kindness, consideration, and sincerity, you will feel more peaceful even when there is no compromise. You will be able to laugh and enjoy life more.

When the outcome occurs you will be content because you stuck to your convictions. You stood up for what you believed is right. In a calm composed manner, without bitterness, you expressed yourself. You will be pleased because you know in the goodness of your heart you gave it all you had. That is all you can do, right? The rest is up to GOD.

However when I say you did your best, means your best. Don't think GOD is going to do you any favors if you slack off and do a mediocre job. Once you do your best you must have TOTAL FAITH (which is discussed in the next chapter) that everything happens for a reason.

Let me elaborate a bit more. Daily task means everyday chores, errands, and events. Chores could be household, yard work or driving your children to school and activities. Errands, we all have them: vehicle maintenance, shopping, post office, dentist, doctor etc. Events could be positive and negative, such as: lunch with a friend or co-worker, school play, movie, out to dinner, playing with your kids, hanging out with friends, kid's sports events, etc.

Negative events would be: paying for a ticket, going to court, housework, having to meet with someone you don't like or they don't like you, or dealing with a painful situation whether it be physical or mental. Like when someone says something to you or does something to you that hurts. Not physically of course but with words. If someone physically hurts you, leave immediately. Get out of the situation; leave the house as quick as you can. Call out for GOD. HE will be there for you. This is not what I am talking about here. That is a whole different degree of circumstances. I am talking about everyday duties.

We see unkindness every day, especially at the store, restaurant, schools, church, while we work on household chores, family gatherings, kids sports events, organization meetings and get this, even when you volunteer.

Now this is a funny story. Since my hubby and I are so blessed with this job, I am able to volunteer my services. Well, I went to a clinic to volunteer and I was asked to call patients to remind them to bring in their stool samples. I didn't have a problem with that; I actually thought it was kind of funny. Anyway, as I was making the phone calls, I came across a very grumpy unkind man who I hope reads this golden book. During our conversation, he asked me, "Where is the clinic?" I told him the approximate location and he asked for the address. I voice to him that this is my first day volunteering and that I wasn't sure. "What do you mean you aren't sure?" He scolded me. "You mean to tell me you are calling me and don't know the address." "Let me talk to your supervisor." I again repeat I am just a volunteer. "So what," he barked back. "You are not doing a good job." If you hold for a second I will get the address. Now, he has been to the clinic before. No, I want to talk to your supervisor; you should know the address before you make these phone calls. I laughed and got my supervisor and he had hung up. I agree, I should have had the address before I made the call and I did get it for the next call but for heaven's sake; was it really necessary to scold and bark at me that way. No wonder why people don't volunteer their services.

People, including me but rarely these days, don't think twice about being rude to waitresses, check-out people, or to others just standing in line. The other day at Wal-Mart, five people were standing in line at customer service. A woman, can't call her a lady, walks right up behind someone getting serviced at the counter and someone says, hey lady here is the line. She says, "this line is shorter". Come on now, she sees everyone else in line. She has the audacity to just walk up in front of everyone. Did she think that no one would see her or catch her? That is so not right and she knows she is not practicing THE GOLDEN RULE. If she was CKCS, this would never have happened. This is why We are writing this golden book and starting this campaign. It will take a conscious effort for everyone. It should be innate but we really have to work at it. Yes, it is actually easier to be rude and selfish but it is so much more peaceful and fun to be CKCS. Again, you will only know it if you try it.

Sure we are all in a hurry but does that give us the right to be rude to people or to treat them with disrespect. How about the ones behind the counter, they are working folk, just like you or me. They would rather be doing something else than putting up with obnoxious people like most of us. White collar or blue, what does it matter; we all are GOD'S children.

> Tangent: Blue collar people are just as smart as white collar. We all have different but great talents. We **all** helped build this world. White collar usually have the great ideas, the blue collar are the ones that do the work and make the white collar look and feel good about the accomplished job. If it weren't for the blue collar, the white collar wouldn't be successful. You see, we are a team that needs each other. Just like the officers need the enlisted to make sure the mission is executed and completed. It takes both, don't you agree?

It also doesn't matter what color our skin is. We are all here to live together in harmony on this planet. Why can't we just be nice to one another EVERYDAY in EVERY situation? It's sad to say that it will be an enormous challenge because as we all know there are always going to be rude people but if most of us continuously practice being CKCS every waking moment then they too will see no matter how they irk us; we stay in control and continue to do everything with love. Ill-mannered people will be blown away at how we handle the most adverse situation and they will eventually want the peace of mind we have. Staying in control is therefore the key to consistency. Wouldn't you agree?

> Tangent: Being in control reminds me of Dave Ramsey. He is the guru that teaches us how to get out of debt which will bring us a better life. He is changing the world on how to have financial peace. He too is a messenger from GOD. He teaches us discipline and has

taught many of us to change the way we spend. He makes it fun to stay in control and pay off our credit cards. I know because that is what my husband and I are doing and it is fun. Of course, it is what you make it. Just listen to his radio show and listen to how many people ate beans and rice, then call in to scream they are debt free. Well, while Dave Ramsey is working on your financial peace; I want to help you work on your inner peace. I highly recommend his book *The Total Money Makeover* and radio show. It's just discipline, retraining and controlling your actions while having fun. Isn't it fun to accomplish goals?

First, you must recognize there is a problem. You must listen and be aware of the way you treat others. You must admit that you are being unkind to others and that you are not practicing THE GOLDEN RULE or doing much of anything with love.

Then you must really want a happier, more peaceful content life which will force you to stay in control and consistently work on these golden skills to gain financial and inner peace. I constantly have to work at both areas in my life, but it gets easier and easier because now I don't have to think about it as much. It's not yet automatic but every day it gets easier and easier just like any skill I work on.

YOU MUST WANT IT!

Once you want it then you will want to work at it, process it, work at it some more until it becomes a habit; a pleasant habit. It's taken me over ten years but I get better and better every day. The reward is remarkably enlightening and I want you to have the same golden feeling I do when I practice THE GOLDEN RULE. I want you to feel how wonderful it feels when I do everything, as much as possible, with love. The feeling is so hard to explain. It's like floating on a cloud, even though I don't know what that feels like.

**It's almost as great as courting but
you are in love with yourself. WOW!**

Incorporate these golden skills into your everyday life and you will have this incredible physical and mental feeling.

May I suggest you start with something as simple as sharing a smile to everyone in your family. Tell them one thing that you appreciate about them; just one. Ask yourself, when was the last time you compliment husband, wife, son, daughter, sister, brother or friend. Find something and be sincere about it. Do it today and take note of the response you get. If you get a "what do you want now", then you know that you haven't shown that person that you appreciate them. Everyone needs to be recognized, loved and needed. EVERYONE! Try it, it is fun. Much more on this later in Chapter 7 in Pay it Forward.

Just like a carpenter, gardener, electrician, homemaker or whatever skill you want. You must first want it and work at it, work at it some more and you will get better and better at it.

First, become aware of how often you are unkind and/ or sincerely kind in the course of a day. For one week, take a look, really be cognizant of your words, tone, body language, actions and reactions when you speak to everyone. I met a woman yesterday; her husband used to call her lightning tongue because she would strike at everyone in a mean way. Most of us get ticked off so quickly and it last too long. Some stay mad for hours. Me, I am working on trying to get over whatever upset me within the hour; depending on the severity of the issue. It used to take me days, then it took me just a day. Now that I have become consciously aware; I don't want to be immobilized that long. Thanks to Dr. Wayne Dyer for teaching me that skill and my Marine for tolerating me. Just remember the faster you get over it; the quicker you can get on with being happy.

Once you recognize that you aren't CKCS, you can get working toward peace of mind with these ideas. I want to express to you how hard I consistently have to work at being The Better Person every day and how you can do the same.

The other day, I was doing my husband a favor and going to pick up a money order for work. He works extremely hard, he is on call 24 hours a day so I enjoy helping him. However, I had just shopped earlier in the day and I really just wanted to go to the front of the store and get out quickly. Well, I asked him, does he need anything else? Bless his heart, he is trying to quit smoking again and he asked me to get him some orange juice. Dummy me, thoughtlessly responds with, I just went shopping earlier and I don't want to shop again. He responds kindly, Ok Honey, I understand. What a jerk I am. Driving to the store I felt guilty and realized I am not practicing what I am writing. I didn't do that with love, and I did fail in my heart. See how I had to think about it; which I call processing. It was inconsiderate of me. I didn't practice THE GOLDEN RULE, and I definitely did not do everything, anything for that matter, with love; not one bit. I bought the juice and apologized. Later that night I kindly rubbed his feet.

But why does it take such an effort to be kind. The only explanation I have is because Eve ate the apple:

> **Genesis 3: 15:**
> **And I will put enmity between you and the woman, and between your offspring and hers?**

Is that why most people hate snakes? Hmm. I also think there is more to this message. It might be to inform us that we will all be enemies from that moment on. I interpret this be GOD'S message that we will all continuously hurt each other. So, without blaming Eve, because

> **I don't believe in blaming anyone.**
> **I just believe in fixing it, right boys?**
> **I instilled this in my three sons**

Thus the only way we can fix this is to practice THE GOLDEN RULE by being CKCS. Again, this may sound too powerful for me to say but I have been told by GOD to tell you I have been chosen to bring back THE GOLDEN RULE.

Wow, even I had a hard time writing that. For me to say something as strong as I have been chosen, scares the daylights out of me. But I committed myself to have TOTAL FAITH and my journal is my confirmation of the work that GOD has asked me to do. It's funny how my life is moving just as GOD planned it. The whole thing is mind boggling. Thank you GOD for this opportunity. "YOU'RE WECOME", HE JUST SAID.

Some of you may think I might be schizophrenic and I am hearing voices like my mother. Yes, she was diagnosed with schizophrenia. What is exciting to me; is I don't care what those people think. For the first time in my life, since I have committed myself to do this. I don't really care about many things because I let go and let GOD. All I know for sure, is I am taking control, making my life for the better, and giving others the opportunity to do so as well. Thus, for those who take Our advice and consistently practice THE GOLDEN RULE and make an effort to do everything with love that they too will be The Better Person and live a happier, peaceful and content life.

It is funny how people react to Our philosophy. Those with GOD, totally agree, with an AMEN sister. The analytical ones, who are also blessed with GOD'S gifts usually have a different opinion; which they are entitled to. They normally pause and respond with; it sounds good but it doesn't always work that way. Sure it does, if you want it to. Let me demonstrate how it will always work.

Most of the time it's easier to be kind and loving when you are happy and joyful, isn't it? However to do everything in a loving manner even if you are hurt, angry or sad is the challenge. Everything includes your body language, physical action, voice inflection, facial expressions and thoughts. All of these reactions to the subject at hand are equally important. Every thought is particularly imperative because your thoughts bring about your actions. If you are consciously aware and think about every word and action you make, you will take notice if you are practicing THE GOLDEN RULE. In other words, when you are in a predicament you must force yourself to think how you would like to be treated if you were in their shoes.

Each thought must be committed to
THE GOLDEN RULE.

At that moment you will know that you did your very best and therefore cannot in any way be wrong. Therefore, you win and they win too. Sure you might not get the desired outcome or you may have to compromise, eat your words, or even be temporarily ashamed. But again, if you do everything with love you will feel better knowing that in your heart, you did the best you absolutely could and that should be all that really matters. What truly matters is when you are able to look in the mirror and say, I did my best GOD; the rest is up to YOU. Or if you are a non-believer, still, if you do your best the rest is up to the universe or whatever you believe. Are you able to do this every day? GOD, I and the person you are with wants you to at least try.

Here is a great example of trying to be The Better Person. It's a very long story but I wanted to show you how I process negative junk in my life and I hope this helps you in troubled times. I am dealing with a situation right now as I write this. I am going to demonstrate how difficult it is to be The Better Person, how I process and process my pain but I am also going to express how wonderful it feels when I get through this because I did everything with love thus, I will not fail.

I was once close to someone dear to my heart. At least I thought so. When they would come over, we would hang out together and watch movies. Often times this person would race to my lap, just like children race to the car to get into the front seat. I would stroke their hair and nurture them by caressing, soothing, or rubbing something if it hurt while we watched tv or told me how their week went. I love

34

this person very much as if they were my own child and I would try to treat them as so. We would cook together, play games together, take plenty of pictures and just hung out. Mary, Mary, come see this or I am saving this movie for just me and you, I would remember.

Our most special moments were when we would go in my bedroom and get up on the bed and have "pillow" talk. Just lie there and catch up on the week, month and sometimes the year's events. We would talk for hours, laughing, crying, me mostly, but we had our very special moments. At least I thought so. I know I said that twice, it is because I am so hurt at this moment.

These next few days are very special days, a life time event is about to occur for this person. I was not only not invited but asked not to come because of a "junk" squabble that happened in the last year.

Now comes The Better Person part and this is how I process my pain. I am so hurt. I am doing better because a little time has past. I used to cry like a baby. You know the kind of cry where your stomach hurts and you feel like throwing up. Now, I just have pains in my heart. Strange, how you can actually feel pain in the heart when your heart is broken. Anyway, being The Better Person right now is so hard. At this moment I could write a letter to the person that hurt me and express how they hurt me and try to temporarily darken their very special day. Or I could be The Better Person and write and tell them how proud I am and congratulate them. Or do nothing and pretend it never happened. Here is what I wrote because I truly am working on being The Better Person and it feels good. Not great at this moment while I process; yet, good, that I didn't rant and rave about how this hurt me. I have more peace of mind going this route than if I chose to be ugly about it. It has been rewritten a little to protect the person.

Dear so and so,

First and foremost, CONGRATS!! YOU DID IT. You did it with full force and pride. For whatever it is worth; I am so proud of you. You made a HUGE step and I wish I was there to do our hug. I wanted so much to share with you what you went through at the notorious school. You always told me from the day we met that you could do anything you put your mind to and you did it even with physical challenges others don't have. I know you will always be able to do anything you put your mind to because you have incredible drive and ambition. YOU GO!!!!!
You were right. This is your day and your family's day and I wasn't there because I wanted this day to be EXTREEMLY special for you and them. I didn't want anyone to be uncomfortable with my presence. My heart is/was there while you got your recognition because I remember how you shared with me your excitement when you were going to join that school. You are always welcome in my home, in my life but if you choose not to; I will treasure our memories, our secrets and our hugs for the rest of my life.

I love you more than you can imagine,
Mary

I will however, express to that person, at the right moment, how this hurt me so. I will also respect their decision and hope we will someday soon develop a close relationship once again. I am patient and kind just as GOD asked me to be. This will be my mantra as I go through this. I will also express to them my feelings as needed. I too worked at making life comfortable for those involved. Credit goes where credit is deserved. I won't however rehash the ugly night that caused this to begin with. There is no reason to go backwards. The situation was blown out of proportion and it happened just the way it was supposed to. Handling this situation with love was extremely large of me.

Now that is truly being The Better Person. Even though this has hurt me so, I can still say that they are beautiful people. I love them so.

See, I could go off on the person that hurt me. I could have called them names and expressed to them how much I hated what they did. Again, I get a pat on the back for being The Better Person. Only those who are or have been in my situation can appreciate what I am doing and how I am handling it.

Ok, it is now 15 hours later since I wrote the last few paragraphs and I am crying, hurting. I just got back from a wonderful vacation with my son. I will be strong and with love I will get through this painful night. It is now 3am. Yes, just like you I hurt but fight with love. I am strong I keep telling myself. I will let go and let GOD. I will be patient, kind and stay busy. Staying busy is the easiest way to not hurt. I will keep busy tomorrow and I will be as strong as I can be. I will accept my feelings; if I cry; that is ok. I will cry more and the day will soon be over. You might not cry as

took my license and my debit card and I called him with a piss poor negative attitude because I was crushed that I wasn't with him. I had told myself earlier that I wasn't going to call him. You know how we do that girls, don't you? Anyway, I got through my day because I stayed focus. Hurt but yet stayed focus on keeping busy with work. Now it is the evening and I am better. Still bummed out but got through it today. It is out of my control and I always said, don't get upset with things that are out of our control.

See how hard it is to be The Better Person. I know it is easier just to raise hell and be mean. However, when all the mean words have been exchanged, what does that solve. Thus, is it really worth it to get mad, yell or not yell but say ugly words to the one that hurt you? Oh, I told her or him. Does it feel better now that "you told them"? Me, I feel junker (that is my word) because I know there is a better way. That is why I try very hard not to waste my energy with being mean or angry. I'm too old to not have peace of mind. It is just a choice. I am teaching myself to not sweat the small stuff.

It is actually more stressful when I bicker back and forth so I just bite my tongue, let go, let GOD and go about my day.

I had to put that in bold because I know I will have to read it again and again when this type of situation comes back up; because it will reappear. Don't get me wrong. I do express my feelings and I don't allow people to step on me but I say it gently which will give them no reason to be mean back to me.

Tomorrow will be better because I have a clean house and did my nails and I am going to look good and feel great for work tomorrow. Knowing that I did my best to keep calm with this extremely painful situation gives me peace of mind. I even just smiled. Thank you GOD for your help through this. YOU'RE WELCOME MARY

I just got up and noticed that my Marine didn't call me to say good night last night. That is one of our love rules. When we are away, we are to call each other to say goodnight. The first one who goes to bed is the first one to call. I waited for his call. That upset me and I text him and let him know. He called me to apologize. I was not happy but got over it because I am not sweating the small stuff and it is all small stuff. Not another unnecessary word said. I continue to be The Better Person. It hurts still but that is part of life and it is not his fault.

Well, it is now a week later. I just haven't had time to write. I am feeling great. When my Marine came home; we really missed each other because I was on vacation prior to him leaving. I chose not to ask any questions about the event because it would make me angry and the hurt would start all over again. We discussed very little about the day. I didn't ask the details. It wasn't necessary. I have let go and let GOD. I wanted to ask. Some women self-inflict pain by asking questions to hurt themselves further.

Ask yourself when you are in a situation like I have described or any situation that makes you uncomfortable, angry or hurt. How much do you really need to know? Would it really make you feel better if you knew all the details? My goal is to have peace of mind and a loving fun relationship with my husband. He didn't do anything wrong. He is not having an affair with anyone. He is experiencing his life the way he wants to and I am not interfering. When we first met, we agreed that you live your life, I live mine and we share ours together. He always told me. "If I know the rules, I can play the game."

My point here was two things. I wanted to share with you; I am human and have been selfish at times. Life was and is a constant struggle. However, ever since GOD told me to do everything with love and I couldn't fail, my life changed. I hope it does the same for you.

Here is another every day situation that being The Better Person is such a great feeling. This one is much easier because it involves strangers not loved ones. My husband and I take our vehicles to different repair shops to get our oil changes and other services. Well, the shop that I go to doesn't sell tires and I needed four new tires. We drive almost 200 miles a day. My Marine suggested quite kindly and offered to buy me my tires from the people he goes to. The owner is a Veteran and we try to keep our business local and with Veterans first. I drove off with four great tires. A couple of months down the road, I thought I should rotate my tires for whatever reason. His shop said that they would do it for free since we bought the tires there. Shortly after my rotation, I notice a noise that got worse as I drove it throughout the week. So I took it back and they said that they are new tires and they need to ware down. Ok, so over the months, it got worse, not better. At this point my GPS was bouncing around.

I asked my repair shop about it for months and they said that the tires were cupping. I really didn't understand how or why but they stated it was a manufacturing defect and that I need to return these and get new tires from them.

Now the call to get this problem taken care of; you know darn well they are not going to be happy with giving me new tires. I told her kindly about the situation. Not once getting upset, not once changing my tone to sound like I was angry. I just calmly discussed the issue and that it needed to be resolved. I told her that I would continue to give them my business if they would help me with these junk tires. I applied THE GOLDEN RULE and I also said everything with kindness. Being totally composed, I said that I would like two new tires and I would buy two other new tires. She rolled her eyes and boarder line rudely said that in her 15 years of business that she has never had two defected tires and the reason is not the tires but my car. She said it was the struts, suspension and something else. Well, she was upset with me and told me to go to get the free tires from my repair shop and that they could get them just as easily as she could. I told her that I was going to go to my technicians and have them check out the mechanics of car to see if my car was causing the tires to cup.

The next day I went to my guys. I was greeted before I got to the door. My dealer went out of their way to explain and show me my tire situation. As we were on a test drive, we called the other dealer and spoke to the owner and she apologized and said kindly that they would take care of the problem. Great, I replied. Bet it was because she knew my husband would not return if I didn't get the best service. It might not be because I was kind and practiced THE GOLDEN RULE. But I demonstrated to her throughout this ordeal that I was trying to be The Better Person and I hope that with my kindness and consistent kindness that she realized she was being unkind to me and she would switch her tone because I didn't give her a reason to get upset with me or be unkind.

I could have had a piss pour attitude and probably would have left angry but not feeling good about myself. Again, since my goal is to be The Better Person, I have to practice what I preach, wouldn't you agree? To me, it's better than the alternative.

Well, when I went to see her, she was kind but somewhat frustrated because she was losing money. I haven't yet told her that I will need four instead of two. To make a long story shorter, she provided me with four new tires; I am going to pay extra for better tires, I don't have a problem with that. She told me that they are cheaper elsewhere but I am loyal to my word; she deserved my business. Sure I need to save money, we all do but right now finances are ok and I want to give her my business because she is helping me.

Now if this was you, how would you handle it? Would you get angry and frustrated and take it out on her? What about your tone of voice, do you sound condescending and argumentative when you speak to people when you are frustrated about something you have to fix, an errand you have to run and you are in a hurry. Do you think it is ok that you are rude to others because you need something yesterday? Weren't you the one who procrastinated? Are you a lightning tongue or do you do your best to do everything with love and practice THE GOLDEN RULE of being consistently kind, considerate and sincere? If you are a lightning tongue, I know you don't have peace of mind. You are probably not enjoying the happiness that I am experiencing and I bet you are not content with your life.

To Summarize:

- Who is The Better Person? You are if you choose to be.
- THE GOLDEN RULE: DO UNTO OTHER AS YOU WOULD LIKE THEM TO DO UNTO YOU OR TREAT OTHERS THE WAY YOU WANT TO BE TREATED
- THE GOLDEN RULE fundamentals: being kind, considerate and sincere (KCS)
- The challenge is to be consistently kind, considerate and sincere (CKCS) in every situation.
- Takes practice, processing, practice. If you can teach IT <u>and</u> practice IT, you have mastered IT and will live a more peaceful, happy and content life.
- The reward for applying THE GOLDEN RULE in your everyday life is a more peaceful, happier and more content life
- Exercise: Share and Tell, a fun way to reminisce
- How were you taught about THE GOLDEN RULE?
- If you are not ready for this golden book that is ok, just keep it for when you are. You will know when that is or please recycle it.
- Are you treating others the way you want to be treated?
- Do every task with love even if outcome is not what you wanted; especially your adversaries; you will feel great.
- Stand up for what you believe in with conviction and kindness
- Do your best; GOD doesn't reward mediocrity

- You must want it; you must want to be consistently kind, considerate and sincere
- Don't be a lightning tongue; speak with kindness, consideration and sincerity
- Don't blame, just fix the problem
- Do everything with love when you are angry. Watch your body language, your physical action, facial expressions, verbal and non-verbal language
- Don't ask unnecessary questions that you know are going to hurt you unless you absolutely need to know.

CHAPTER 2

WORK HARD & HAVE TOTAL FAITH

The best way to explain what TOTAL FAITH means is to tell you the story how I discovered IT and how I am experiencing IT as I write this golden book. I had just moved to Orlando in 2002, in love, and excited about my new life. Blessed with the same job and a temporary salary, I was ready to jump on my next stepping stone or as some would say start a new chapter in my life. Of course life didn't go as smoothly as I had planned; it rarely does, sound familiar?

This stone actually had a crack in it and I had to fix it but didn't know how and I became quite depressed. My sales were very slow because I had lost my confidence and I wasn't focused on my job. I was in another state; scared but persistent. I continued to get up everyday at 5:30am and worked in the humid 100 degree weather, the freezing 30 degree weather and every temperature in between. I slacked off more than I should have at first because I was so used to my success in Hawaii. Thus, I wasn't doing my best and my sales were lacking. I took my frustrations out on my Marine and end up crying myself to sleep.

Until one day, I spoke to my Angel. He was the warehouse manager of one of the largest department stores in the US.

Let me go off on another tangent if you don't mind because I want you to be exposed to GOD'S Angels and how they are apparent in your life. You see, GOD lends us HIS Angels when we attempt and especially if we commit to being The Better Person. Thus, if you do your absolute best at what you are trying to accomplish, practice THE GOLDEN RULE and put effort to doing everything with love; HE will share even more of HIS Angels with you. Since I started to be The Better Person HE has shared many of HIS Angels with me. These Angels are everyday people that help other people just when they need it the most. This person could be a temporary friend. Ever heard of the saying, "People come into your life for a reason, season and or life time." Well if they come into your life for a reason or a season, most likely they are one of GOD'S Angels. HIS Angels are lent to me just at the right time. GOD knows exactly when to send them to you and how long to lend them to you. I am sure you have experienced some of GOD'S Angels in your lifetime. I too am one of GOD'S Angels. I have helped so many people and with my golden book I will help millions more. I also am so proud to say that I also have helped many of our Veterans, single women and broken families. Are you one of GOD'S Angels? What an honor it is, isn't it? Wouldn't you like to be one of GOD'S Angels more often? I am sure you have at one time acted as one of GOD'S Angels. If not, you might learn the teaching in this golden book and help people more often. My Marine is one of GOD'S Angels. Go back for a moment and think about who were the Angels in your life. You might want to look them up and thank them. Please share your angel story on my website.

Now I will get back to my story. Intimidated by this executive, I faced my fear and did everything I could to get to meet with David after I read the book: *Face your Fears and Do It Anyway* written by: Susan Jeffers PHD. A book I highly recommend to anyone who is intimidated by people and wants to get over it. You can't just read it once. That is another book that you must memorize.

When I met him, he told me he has no idea how I got an appointment to see him because he doesn't allow new vendors to meet with him. I wondered why too. He told me he would give my products a try. I was in the door.

After pounding the pavement for weeks, I fell into a depression because my sales were still not going as they should and a bunch of other bad things were happening in my life. It was the end of the month and I needed another sale to prove my worth to my company. Persistently, I picked up the phone to call my customers. I called David who is definitely one of GOD'S Angels. He answered so kindly, "hello Mary". I could feel him smiling and I said, "Hi David, "I just want to take a minute of your time and tell you how grateful I am to have your business." He cheerfully says, "You are welcome, the guys really like your products. In fact I want you to send me two cases a week, starting today." WOW! I couldn't wait to tell my manager. That was a great order.

At that moment, I don't know why I had the nerve to asked him but I did, "David, why is it that you are always so happy all the time?" He said, "Because I have been saved and I have TOTAL FAITH in GOD." "Well, I too have been saved." I responded, "I too have faith in GOD." "<u>Yeah, but do you have TOTAL FAITH?</u>" He exclaimed. I am really not sure how the conversation went after that because I was struck by awe. I do know that I got off the phone and yelped, "that's IT!" "I don't have TOTAL FAITH. I don't truly believe that GOD will provide for me and that everything will be ok". I was living in fear not love. My loving spirit had dissipated during my move. I was angry, ugly and not practicing THE GOLDEN RULE. Then the tears came pouring down. I told my Marine, about my remarkable experience. From that day on I not only gave my life to serve GOD, but I discovered TOTAL FAITH. It's elating to TRULY believe I will never have to worry about how I am going to "make it" ever again. WOW!! To TRULY know that GOD will ALWAYS provide for me with shelter, food and what ever else is necessary to live and then some, is such a stress relief. How do you spell relief, G O D! (Thank you Rolaids) Now, that is TOTAL FAITH. Can you imagine a stress free life or at least a minimum stressful life? I have it and so can you.

It will only happen when you TOTALLY believe that no matter what happens in your life, GOD will provide for you. You will never go hungry. HE will provide you of what you need. You cannot have just some faith in GOD. In order for you to reach the height that I am at right now you must truly believe in TOTAL FAITH.

For those of you who don't believe in GOD. I feel for you because it is much easier to go through life with HIM than without HIM. Again, this golden book is not about getting you to believe in GOD. That will come on your own time. If you don't believe in THE ALMIGHTY, then put all your faith in yourself or whatever force you believe in. That's ok too. You will come out with similar results if you do your very best and work hard, believe you can do whatever you put your mind to. You too should be able to accomplish your endeavors. However, with doing it with love, and adding the kind touch of THE GOLDEN RULE you will not only accomplish personal and possibly financial success but you will at that time experience the more peaceful, happy and content life I am talking about.

Yes, I did say, you don't have to believe in GOD. It's just easier to have GOD to talk to while you struggle, push on and then prevail. Again, believing in GOD is your prerogative.

Nevertheless, I highly suggest you at least explore your spirituality and GOD and truly search for the meaning of why you are here on this Earth because it is so exciting when you discover your destiny. However, if you can do this on you own; more power to you. I just want you to find peace of mind, be truly happy with who you are and to be content with your life.

You know how people say they have been saved. You don't have to get baptized or be born again in order to do your best with love and have TOTAL FAITH. My husband who is a confident Marine was baptized and confirmed. He wasn't saved again. However, he always does his best and truly has TOTAL FAITH that everything will be ok; even at the worst times in his life. For the most part he practices THE GOLDEN RULE. He always works hard at trying his best and believes in himself. Any boss will tell him his work ethic is better than they ever expected from him. Boy was I wrong. I used to think he was just a really cute dumb biker dude. In fact most biker dudes are pretty smart. He is consistently kind, most of the time considerate and he is very sincere. Furthermore, he is extremely generous. When we could barely pay our bills; you could come over and eat for free. He would buy our friends and family member's dinner and drinks even when we knew we shouldn't. He could do so because he always has TOTAL FAITH. That's all you have to do, just believe that GOD, the Universe or whatever you believe in will always provide you with what you need if you do your best. You must believe it though. You will know when you truly do believe in TOTAL FAITH because you will FEEL more peaceful, happy and content in your life. A huge burden will be lifted. The feeling is remarkable. It's like being in love all the time. Courtship or when you first fall in love is an incredible feeling, isn't it? Well when you do your best with love and learn to truly have TOTAL FAITH, you will have that feeling but it isn't temporary. It stays as long as you keep TOTAL FAITH.

> ***If you do your part which is to work hard,
> practice THE GOLDEN RULE and
> do everything with love while at the
> same time, have TOTAL FAITH;
> GOD will provide for you.***

Notice I put the above statement in bold, italics and underlined it. Because this should be written on your wall, kept in your purse, and be your mantra. Memorize these lines and just doing it will bring you a more peaceful, happy and content life. Try it for yourself because that is the only way you will know.

Are you at peace and as happy and as content in your life as I am? If not, then what do you have to lose to try any of these ideas. You don't have to do all of what We are asking you to try. Just try out one of Our suggestions at first and if you like it then work on the next. If you don't like the feeling, then pass this golden book on to someone who might or at least recycle it please. Then again, if you do like it then please pass this on to a mean person. Cause like the bumper sticker says, "mean people suck".

Getting back to how I discovered TOTAL FAITH. The only stress I experienced was when I had doubt; the opposite of TOTAL FAITH. Yes, I had doubt many times after my Angel spoke to me but nothing compared to the past because my life took off in an extremely positive direction after that day. Life is great because I practice THE GOLDEN RULE, do everything with love and know what TOTAL FAITH truly is.

My doubt came when we moved to South Carolina. I had to start all over again, knocking on doors in a new territory. I remember when we were eating left over concession food from our concession trailer and saying, I'm scared, how will we pay our mortgage? HE ANSWERED, I'M NOT GOING TO TAKE YOUR HOUSE SILLY, I JUST GAVE IT TOO YOU. YOU ALSO NEED YOUR CAR TO WORK FOR ME. As I showed you earlier, my journal entry said, JUST KEEP DOING WHAT YOU ARE DOING, SOMETHING BIG IS COMING. Shortly thereafter, a check arrived in the mail from the IRS. It was for $7,500 for the first time home-buyer credit. The timing was planned just exactly as GOD had planned it. Once again, HE provided because I obeyed HIS command.

consistent that is the biggest challenge. HE also appreciates my effort because HE knows that we are not perfect and as long as we try we will be rewarded.

Thus, it is imperative you have TOTAL FAITH to obtain a happier, more peaceful, content life in this greedy, confused unloving world. How you obtain TOTAL FAITH is something you have to work on yourself; I cannot give IT to you. It is changing your mind set and thought process and totally believing **without a doubt** that you will be ok no matter what. All you have to do is ask GOD and listen to your INNER VOICE. It's not easy to tune in to your INNER VOICE especially if you are hurting, suffering or just having a really bad year. All I can tell you is, believe TOTALLY that you are here for a reason, figure out that reason and really start living.

Discovering TOTAL FAITH might be one of your biggest worthwhile challenges. For some, like my Marine, it is natural to believe it will be ok even if you are broke or hurting. They are the fortunate. For others, they might temporarily lose hope, get lazy, drink or become addicted to something that will temporarily let them escape and/or get depressed and just sit around and watch television or play video games all day. Again, that life can get old. There is and can be so much more to your life if you want it. Go ahead if you want, waste days, weeks, years laying around and feeling sorry for yourself. Or get up and make a change and help yourself so you can eventually help others. It is only up to you, isn't it?

If you are depressed right now but want to enjoy a more peaceful, happy and content life then let me give you a jumpstart. Let's pretend for a minute. Close your eyes right now, pretend my fingers are like jumper cables and I am sticking them in your ear. Now pretend to cough because you are having a hard time smiling. Cough again because you just can't get started. Now remember my fingers are in your ear. You better start smiling or laughing or I am going to wet them and stick them in your ear again. If that doesn't work, I will have to blow in your face and you don't want that. Laugh silly, it's funny.

Let's take a look at those who have TOTAL FAITH in GOD. Notice how happy they are? They almost look like dolphins, where they are always smiling, glowing. You can hear it in their voice, even on the phone. It's easy to spot a person who has TOTAL FAITH because there is something so special about the way they carry themselves, speak and their actions are kind. Like last night, I walked into a house and I could just tell these lovely people love GOD as much as I do. They were so blessed. They had a typical middle class home. When I shook her hand, I could feel something touch my heart and she said the same about me. I found out later that she works forty hours a week, takes care of her grandchildren and husband, and bakes cakes from scratch for the elderly free of charge. They are super delicious! She was so kind to give me her last two pieces. She doesn't need this golden book. She already has TOTAL FAITH, she has discovered why she is here and she continually tries her best making sure she practices THE GOLDEN RULE with love. When was the last time you did something for someone free of charge and not expect anything back? Go ahead, try it. Give something to anybody today. Anything, it doesn't matter what it is, just do a random act of kindness for one person, anyone. It's such a great feeling when you do. However, you will not know unless you try it. Do you like to cook, sew, or garden? Reach out and help the elderly, you will be old someday and wouldn't you like it if someone came to visit with a homemade pie, cookies, or cake. Or if you like to sew how about making a homemade pillow or throw blanket. If you enjoy gardening take some of your fresh cut flowers or a small plant they can nurture and just give someone a reason to smile.

Don't you want to laugh out loud and smile more than you frown? Yeah, yeah, laughter is the best medicine but do you really believe that. I do. I love to laugh and I laugh out loud. Last night my hubby and I went out to dinner and I laughed out loud. I might have been a little loud but who cares. Laughing is fun, especially if it is from your belly. My favorite thing to do is to laugh so hard my stomach hurts or tears come to my eyes. I watch Ellen as much as possible. When I am down I go to my self help books and then I watch or read anything that will make me laugh. I save the funny emails just for those days too.

Now on the other hand, I went to get my hair done the other day at a Cosmetology school and my hair stylist almost convinced me that she loved GOD with all her heart and how GOD is her driving force and how she has faith. She had me convinced that she was The Better Person until she started to talk stink about people in the shop. I don't think she would like it if others talked stink about her, do you? I know I hate it when I find out that someone said something negative about me because I really do try to practice THE GOLDEN RULE. Someone once told me:

**It is none of your business
what others say about you.**

That's so true but I still don't like it. Nobody likes negative junk said about them, so why do we do it.

See when you have TOTAL FAITH; you won't want to talk stink about others. You will want to make this a better place for EVERYONE; even for those that are difficult to get along with. You will see life in rose colored glasses. Better yet you will create you own colored glasses, mine are yellow turning gold, because your perception in every aspect of your life will change. Just start with THE GOLDEN RULE and then do everything with love because once you do that you will most likely see that what I am saying here is true and then you will go on your journey to obtain TOTAL FAITH which will put you on the path to a more peaceful, happy, and content life.

I feel for people that don't have the loving spirit that they could experience. Now that I practice THE GOLDEN RULE, when people talk stink about others or say negative things, I make an effort to turn it around. For example someone tells me so and so likes to always be in charge, bossy, and is on a "power trip" or a person who is called a micro manger can be derogatory but if you change your perception and look at it as if they just want to help you, teach you to be the best you can be then that person is no longer ugly in your eyes, right? He or she could actually be your hero. Thus, you must be as stubborn as them. Isn't it more peaceful to have a hero than to have a control freak? It's just a matter of how you control the way you look at things; your perception. See more on perception in Chapter 5.

Of course every situation is different. By all means, stand up for yourself, without raising your voice and speak firm but kind. When the Veteran was yelling at me the other day and telling me to get out of his house. I kept saying to him. The last thing I wanted to do was to piss him off. I was there to help Veterans and that I appreciate his service to our country and that he had the guts to join and I appreciate that he protected my freedom some way, some how. I told him that I was just following policy and that wouldn't he do the same at his job. I stayed calm with love and he noticed I was there to help him not hurt him. With my golden skills to be CKCS, I was able to help him. Yet just recently found out he had a credit issues and that his loan wasn't approved; probably because he wasn't honest with himself or me. See how GOD takes care of things.

Don't you think most humans want to have TOTAL FAITH but they don't know how to get, have and keep IT. They want to have IT but they are not staying focused on how to get IT or on how to keep IT. They go about their everyday life, mostly caring only about themselves. Since I have reached the pinnacle of having TOTAL FAITH, I find that I care more about others than myself and it is so rewarding. For example, for Christmas this year I could have spent money on myself. I could have replaced my stained ugly carpet, bought me more new clothes or more things for my house or hired someone to help me rake my leaves or many other things but instead I helped others and bought three children I have never met, toys for their Christmas, I provided heat for a desperate woman and her family and I also was able to buy two bikes for two kids I don't even know.

All We ask is that you take a conscious thought and/or prayer and ask GOD to help you obtain TOTAL FAITH. HE will answer you. You just have to be still and listen to HIS answer. HE told me to tell you, if you do your absolute best to practice THE GOLDEN RULE, HE will respond to you. I'm not sure how because that is between you and HIM. That's pretty bold of me to write that but that is what HE told me to tell you. When you do obtain TOTAL FAITH; please write me and tell me your story. My website is:

bethebetterperson.org.

This world, especially our Nation, is in really bad shape right now and having TOTAL FAITH & THE GOLDEN RULE are going to re-spirit it. However, I need your help. The reward is, heavy sigh, so remarkable. Are you in?

I know this may not be relevant but for some strange reason, just recently my favorite color changed from red to yellow and now I am moving toward gold. Why, I have no idea. Ooops, yes I do. It is because it is my job to bring back THE GOLDEN RULE. Get this, I was at Lowe's picking out my carpet and after I had selected it and was in the process of ordering it the clerk told me the name of carpet. Guess what it is called, THE GOLDEN RULE. The color is rosewood. What are the chances of that? To top that off, I have been looking for a kitten for weeks; I lost my talking cat last year. Guess what color it is, golden. Not only that he has an incredible personality . . . . Hmmmm, coincidence, I don't think so. You see, everything really does happen for a reason but you won't grasp that phenomenon until you attain TOTAL FAITH.

Thus if you always do your best and try as much as possible to have a positive attitude toward yourself and how your life will work out, then life will get better. You just have to truly believe it. Doing your best and having a positive attitude are elements of TOTAL FAITH. They go hand in hand. Because you cannot slack off, expecting others to give to you so you can live comfortably. Could you really have a peaceful, happy, and live a content life if someone did all the work for you and you just laid around eating, sleeping and just thinking about yourself? Is that fulfillment? Sure it sounds good if you win the lottery or born royal but even they won't truly live a peaceful, happy, and content life unless they find their purpose and give back. Furthermore, you cannot be a pessimist and have TOTAL FAITH. That is an oxymoron. So what would you rather be a grumpy, negative, inconsiderate person or a happy, joyful, kind, caring, loving human? Keep in mind, the choice is yours. Thank you Bill.

Unfortunately it took me a long time to reach the ability to have TOTAL FAITH. That is why We are writing this. We don't want it to take you and our entire population that long. GOD knows that right now with the shape of our nation, we need this now. How you are to attain TOTAL FAITH is difficult to teach you. This is not a how to obtain TOTAL FAITH book. That is your journey. I don't know how you are going to do this. I do know and I might sound like a broken record but repetition is how we learn. If you do your best daily, practice THE GOLDEN RULE every day, do everything with love not fear and ask GOD; HE will grant you the pleasure of TOTAL FAITH. When you ask, make sure you listen and do what HE says. Always listen to your INNER VOICE. Read, research, get a journal and figure out what you like to do, your special talent/s, we all have at least one; then start living. What is your favorite thing to do? How can you share that with others? You can do anything you put your mind to but you must believe you can first. You can dooo it, my youngest son would say.

This is amazing. My Marine went to a meeting this weekend for work and he came home and seemed disappointed. Like most men, he didn't like to share what he was feeling. We talked but just about the facts. You know how most guys are. I went to work yesterday and he calls me to tell me he resigned his position of manager and wanted to step down because his numbers were junk and the job is just too demanding and stressful. He was miserable. I support anything he chooses; that is what a good wife does. More on this in Be The Better Partner; coming soon. The last thing I want is for him to be miserable and his health was my concern. However, I was upset that he didn't discuss it with me first and I told him so. Well, GOD told me to write in my journal a couple of days earlier that HE will take care of my Marine. Sure enough HE did; GOD wouldn't let him resign as manager. Remember this isn't his money, it's GOD'S and HE has plans with this money. Later that day my Marine got a phone call from the owner of the company and the owner told my Marine he was doing a great job and that he doesn't want him to resign his position. Another boss told him he is family to that company and that once you are in; you cannot get out. My Marine smiled and he is going to march on as manager. He just needed to be reassured that he was doing a good job. Don't we all? The main reason he wanted to step down was because he thought that someone else could do a better job; he felt bad because the owner was loosing money because his loan officers weren't doing their job. Now that is The Better Person if you ask me, wouldn't you agree?

Again, his success is not about him. It's about how we are soon going to buy a bunch of billboards to campaign GOD'S GOLDEN RULE. Call me crazy. I am just listening to my INNER VOICE. Talk about an example of TOTAL FAITH. Not only that, it is snowing today so all our work is postponed; which gives us a couple of days off to regroup. It's wonderful how everything works out if you work hard and have TOTAL FAITH!

Stop right now, ask HIM. GOD, I have faith but how do I get to have TOTAL FAITH like Mary is writing about here? Talk to HIM, call it prayer but just have a chat like HE is your friend or a teacher who you want to learn from.

While your talking to HIM, make sure you thank HIM for all that you have now. If you don't know how to do that, please read the next chapter. Better yet, let's see if you do know how to thank HIM. Go ahead, do it your way first. Thank HIM, and then ask HIM what you can do for all HE has given you. Then after you read the next chapter, compare it to how you should thank HIM.

Don't worship HIM,
Thank HIM
and then get to work for HIM.

To Summarize:

- When you have TOTAL FAITH; GOD will always provide for you.
- Memorize this
- *If you do your part which is to work hard, do your best at your job, practice THE GOLDEN RULE and do everything with love while at the same time, having TOTAL FAITH; GOD will provide for you.*
- Must be honest with yourself and others
- Do something for someone without expecting anything back; then ask yourself how you feel.
- Laugh everyday
- You won't talk stink about anyone if you have TOTAL FAITH
- Ask GOD how you can attain TOTAL FAITH

CHAPTER 3

BE NOT ONLY THANKFUL FOR WHAT YOU HAVE, BE GRATEFUL

Let's start with getting out of bed in the morning. I must do things systematically or I get confused. Do you wake up with a smile saying, I am so excited about today because I'm alive and able to get up out of bed. Think about that for a moment. Were you physically able to get out of bed all by yourself? That may not sound like a big deal to most of us but think of the thousands that cannot. Are you grateful that you have two legs and are able to climb out of bed and not crawl? Do you even think about that? Well, our best friend Jimmy just fell out of a tree this past week and he cannot get out of bed at all. What we take for granted. Have you ever taken the time to actually appreciate something most of us think is so ordinary?

Exercise: Stop right now and think about how you got up this morning. Did the alarm go off and you just want to sleep more? If you are like most people and not truly grateful for your life, you would probably want to quickly hit the snooze button and sleep more. Most of us want to be lazy and not go to work. Not Jimmy, more than anything, he wanted to jump out of bed and get to work. Isn't it funny how most of us want the opposite of what we have?

Take this exercise a step further: Don't get up all day. On a day when you don't have to work, stay in bed. Don't read, don't watch tv, don't do anything and pretend you can barely move. If you do you would be in pain. Just lie there all day and think about the thousands that are doing exactly what you are that given moment. Then think about what you would do and how you would act if that did happen to you. Really picture it, have a true visual. Like you are day dreaming but this is not a dream; it is a nightmare. Try it, stay in bed all day. Only get up to go to the bathroom. Have someone bring you something to eat, like broth.

Even another step further: blind fold yourself; do this ALL day and on Sunday. GOD won't mind if you don't go to church as you teach yourself to be grateful that you are alive and able to get up on your own while so many cannot. If you are retired and "feeling sorry for yourself" then do it for a week. Just do it until you know that you WANT to get out of bed every morning and live that day to the fullest. Once you do want to live each day to the fullest then you can figure out what work you can do for the LORD. You could go to my website and see how you can help us bring back THE GOLDEN RULE.

Hopefully the only reason you should want to sleep in is because you were up late the night before and didn't get enough sleep. "YOU CAN SLEEP WHEN YOU ARE DEAD," GOD once told me. Now is the time to enjoy what you have right in front of you, don't you agree?

Just curious, were you able to make a cup of coffee, pour yourself a fresh glass of cold milk, refreshing juice, water or whichever you enjoy this morning? Were you able to have a cold beverage or did you have your refrigerator turned down because you couldn't afford to keep it as cold as you want? If it is winter right now, is it cold in your house and are you wearing layers of clothing and gloves because you cannot afford a pleasurable temperature? As you are drinking that warm or cold beverage, are you really enjoying it, savoring the moment of the fresh smell of that coffee and the feeling of warm coffee going down your throat? The reason I ask is because that is one of my favorite things of the morning; is to have what I call my fufu coffee; French vanilla or hazelnut cream, yum. I especially enjoy the soft jolt coffee gives me to get me going.

Well, when my Marine and I were broke. I would save yesterday's coffee and had to drink it with just milk and sugar, wearing gloves and a hat. Some days we didn't even have milk. Boy do we love our coffee in the morning. What I am saying is, once you have to go without; it sure will be fabulous when you get to have it again. It's the same morning beverage but just taste better because you truly appreciate it now that you know what it's like to not have that luxury. Yes, a cup of warm fresh coffee with fufu in your warm heated home on a cold winter day is a luxury.

So when you get up and while you are waiting for your coffee to perk or as you are taking your first sip of your morning beverage; every once in a while look up and make sure you thank GOD for providing you with such lavishness.

Not everyday of course will we be able to "live in the now" because we are so busy. However, just noticing and taking a conscious awareness of how wonderful your life really is every once in a while, will bring you to a more pleasant, peaceful state of mind. You won't know until you truly experience appreciating what you have. Try it, it is fun!

Another example, turn on the shower to get it hot, then stand there and think about the people who don't have jobs right now; that are not able to take hot showers everyday. Now get in and feel how wonderful the water feels on your body and wash with your favorite soap. I had to use shampoo samples from hotels for soap when we were broke. Don't you love that refreshing feeling when you get to strip the towel off and get dressed because you are warm? Well, think about what it's like when you have a cooler shower and you shiver when you get out because you weren't able to revel in a hot shower on a cold winter day.

The only reason I am keep talking about a hot shower is because I went without my luxurious bath everyday when we were broke. A bath, which I take pleasure in now, was out of the picture back then. Of course I showered but they were like a boot camp showers.

Also, taking your mind off the stress of the upcoming day for a few minutes is more pleasant than taking a shower with hectic demanding pressures of what is to come. Try being thankful first thing in the morning and continue throughout the day until you sound almost ridiculous. That is when you know you are truly grateful. Besides if you are thanking GOD for what you have, you cannot have another thought in your mind at the same time and that helps if you are stressed.

> Tangent: Did you know you cannot have two thoughts at the exact same time? You probably did. It sounds silly to ask but it actually took me a while to grasp this idea, especially when I was stressed out. So, if you think about good, positive things then you cannot, at the exact same time, think about junk negative

stuff. Therefore, it makes total sense to think a positive thought as often as possible which will block any negative unnecessary thought. I say unnecessary because most negative thoughts are unnecessary, agree? This is a tangent but so important for you to not only understand this concept but to work on it if you are stressing.

Ok, now you are getting into your car to go to work. First of all you better truly be grateful you have a job because as I write this, there are over 20 million Americans that are unemployed. That might not be the case if you read this golden book past the publishing date. The years of 2008-2011, as I write this, was the worst recession in history.

USA Today
Foreclosure filings surpassed 3 million in 2008
Foreclosures last year were up 81% from 2007 and 225% from 2006, according to a report out today from RealtyTrac. One in 54 homes received at least one foreclosure filing during the year, RealtyTrac reported

It got worse in 2009-2011. So again, how is your car? Do you have one? Does it run and get you to work so that you can pay your bills and have a roof over your head. Down the street from my home there is an auction lot that has acres and acres of cars, boats, RVs, trucks, etc that are repossessed. It's filled and sold every week. Thus, millions have had there transportation taken away. Do you really appreciate that you have a vehicle? Or are you like most

Americans and just think that's the way it is supposed to be.

I really think the economy works the way it does so that we learn to appreciate what we have. We have a boom in jobs, people spend their money frivolously and then we have bust; unemployment, soup lines, etc. Since we can't balance our finances by our self, GOD has to do it for us.

> This is a tangent for those who make a lot of money. You know who you are. Are you giving enough? How much do you really need to live a luxurious enjoyable life? Of course, make sure you have more than enough if your work were to stop. Yes, you absolutely do deserve the frivolous things you want; you worked hard for it. My question is; is it fulfilling to have, have and have more things than necessary? Ok, what is necessary. That is up to you. You deserve the finer things in life. I too just enjoyed an extreme Valentine's Day ski vacation at the Chetola Resort. Wow, that was fabulous! I too have lived a day or two of the good life. It's fun, but it isn't as fulfilling to me as giving gifts away to children who didn't have anything for Christmas or paying for heat for a single mom and three kids. Sure I know most of you give but what if you gave even more. Besides, did you know the more you give, the more you get? Yeah, but don't do it for the getting. Do like Ellen, do random acts of kindness and buy a single mom a new car when you buy yourself one or a year of groceries. Or pay for someone who needs an operation, schooling, or daycare.

Help people, especially single mothers who are willing to work and need a little help to raise their kids. The ones who are trying to better themselves but are stuck; the ones that you think deserve the help. You were stuck at one time, weren't you? Find someone who was in the same situation as you. Ask me on my website and we will find someone that struggled like you did. You will also be given the opportunity to mentor them. Take some more of your money and time; reach out to help them. The feeling is incredible when you do.

Do you really need 100 pairs of shoes? This just out, nobody but you really cares if every pair of your shoes matched each of your outfits. If others say they do care then they really need to do some soul searching. Sure I love your shoes or your dress; where did you get them is a nice compliment but what is more fulfilling. You know that warm and fuzzy feeling you get when you do something nice for someone. Take a few minutes please and think about the ones who don't have shoes or one nice outfit that they could show off like you show off your wardrobe. It might even help their self-esteem. That would be nice, wouldn't it?

So, here's an idea, the next time you buy a pair of shoes or that dress for over $500.00; or set your own dollar amount. Buy a child a pair as well and maybe a little girl a cute dress so she can feel as cute as you. Or a young boy would surely feel special in his new threads. You too will feel better, especially when you wear your new shoes or new dress. You will be able to tell the story how you not only bought yourself a beautiful pair of shoes and outfit but you put a new pair of shoes on a child. You even went a step further and spiffed up a child. Somewhere in the US there will be a little person smiling and prancing or strutting because she is wearing a new dress or a cool new shirt that you bought and they don't even know you bought it. They don't know but GOD does.

New is better, isn't it? Sure hand me downs are good but there is nothing like a new dress, a new pair of shoes and/or a new outfit for a guy, wouldn't you agree? If you think used is as good as new then why don't you shop at thrift stores. Don't get me wrong please, used is good but new is just better every once in a while.

Just buy a stranger something special once and it will be like eating a Lay's Potato Chips, "you won't be able to eat (help) just one." At first, we will help the families of America. When we help our children first and educate them as well, then they will be asked to Pay It Forward to help the families of other countries. Wow, just think, everyone on our Earth, will eventually have a new pair of shoes. If you are not sure who needs a pair of shoes or a new outfit; please go to my website. There will be a number you can contact

Also, be sure to reach out and help our Veterans, they are the ones that fought for your freedom and they have families that could use a few extra dollars for school supplies, warm

> clothing, school events or help some get their
> teeth fix; or anything. If giving doesn't make
> you feel good, I feel for you.

My point here is, for you to obtain your peace of mind,
to be happy and live your content life you must be **truly
thankful** for everything you have. When you share with
others; you are being grateful in GOD'S EYES. I cannot
express this enough.

If you are only half-ass thankful, you will not feel true
peace of mind. Maybe you don't realize the importance of
peace of mind. Maybe you are not at the stage in your life
to be concerned with peace of mind. I never even heard of it
until after 40 years old. Peace of mind, what is that? When
I was ready my teachers taught me.

Once you TRULY are grateful for what you have, you
will **feel** different about EVERYTHING you do? Once
you consistently practice and are able to teach others these
golden skills, your life will be enriched with more pleasant
loving thoughts almost everyday. It will feel so much better
than just getting up in the morning, drinking a cup of
coffee, taking a shower or driving to work. You will get up
with a smile on your face, not wanting to hit the snooze
button. You will probably not even "need" that cup of
coffee. Me, I am not there yet and don't want to be because
I enjoy my coffee in the morning and walking through my
garden. Your shower could feel like refreshing rain drops if
you let your imagination take you away to a beautiful rain
forest. The soap you use could cleanse your body of stress if
you don't think about anything but how refreshing it feels
as you wash. You might even say, wow, that felt great. Only
if you appreciated that you had hot water will you have a
wow moment. At those instants, when you get out of the

shower or warming up your car, take a few seconds and thank GOD for how fortunate you are. You are blessed that you have hot water and a job, aren't you? As you are getting dressed; make sure you take just another second to thank GOD for your nice clothing. Get to the point, like I am, where I thank HIM all the time; HE might reply you are welcome and ask you to work for HIM.

Like the lady who bakes from scratch. Wow, her cake is better than any store bought or restaurant because it is made from her heart. She bakes so the elderly who don't have the pleasure of enjoying store bought or restaurant desserts; can lavishly enjoy them. She has a regular forty hour a week job that she is thankful for which pays her bills. She doesn't love her job but it is ok because it gives her the money to do what she really enjoys. You would think that she would be too tired to bake but GOD gives her the energy to bake for those that cannot enjoy the bakery cakes that we are so privileged to savor; which fulfills her heart and soul.

Discovering what your gift is and finding out why you are here is your journey. If you are just going to work, coming home and paying the bills, watching tv then you are just existing, aren't you? Do you want to just exist on this planet or do you really want to live?

However, if you have not yet discovered your gift, talent or abilities; it might be that you are here to help me promote THE GOLDEN RULE. Regardless of what it is, you have a purpose. Everyone has a gift, even you. Your life will have so much more meaning after you figure it out.

Finding your purpose reminds me of one of my sons. He is a chunk of love; always smiling but was easily bored growing up. Mom, there's nothing to do and he would get into mischief. My husband at the time, his step father, would get him involved with soccer, basketball, baseball, football, tae-kwando, the saxophone, puzzles, Lego, models, etc, but he was not passionate for any of these activities. Nothing excited my son until his stepfather took him fishing. He loves to fish and hunt; he is extremely good at both.

We literally searched for an activity for him to do when we should have recognized that fishing was hereditary. He loves living in Alaska and fishing and hunting are still his favorite things to do. He consistently practices being The Better Person and generously gives away his fish and game and sincerely helps anyone in his path. He too has a good life because his mother taught him THE GOLDEN RULE and to be The Better Person in any given situation. So can you, once you find out why you are here. Good luck on that journey. Listen to your heart when you ask yourself what do you like to do and what do you do well. There are many books out there to help you find your destiny.

Now you are on your way home from work. Traffic annoys you. Well, try to slow down and enjoy the ride. When traffic is slow or there is an accident causing a traffic jam, I find a good CD and dance, sing and rock out with passion. It passes the time and its fun. You will be jamming with the traffic jam. Ok, most of you are not a drama rockin queen like I am.

However, you are better off; will have more peace of mind if you just accept the traffic and try to have pleasant thoughts about the day. Don't you agree? Maybe think about what went right at work? What could I do better next time? Did I shower people with kindness or was I grumpy and demanding? Doesn't it suck to work with mean people? Did you practice THE GOLDEN RULE today? Did you try, no matter how difficult people were, to be kind to everyone even if they were ugly to you? Of course, stand your ground with your convictions but be kind. Remember, if you did everything with love, you cannot fail because you know in your own heart that you did your very best and that is all you can do. The rest is up to GOD. However, if you lowered yourself and let them get to you and you also became negative, ugly and said unnecessary words and gestures then you really are not doing everything with love, are you?

Let me give you an example. Just last night I went to a Veteran's home and before I got there they read negative information about our company on the internet. Before I could even introduce myself and thank her husband sincerely for his service, she was attacking me with negative mean words, facial expression and body language. She told me I was wasting her time and keeping her from having dinner with her family. Here I was there to save her over $500 a month and approximately $100,000 but she didn't trust me and her eyes were full of fear. I consistently showered her with kindness for over two hours and I must admit I too was getting frustrated and told myself that I don't even want her to have this loan. Then my loving spirit and the golden skill of doing everything with love came back to me, I took a short breath and I repeated my mantra, do everything with love and you cannot fail; do everything with love and you cannot fail. I had to say it a few times throughout the presentation. The rest is up to you GOD. Wow, that was not fun but a challenge and I like challenges. They were rolling their eyes, laughing at me, and expressing to me what a scam we were. I had all my evidence that we were a great company providing a remarkable service for Veteran's only and I don't know if I convinced her because I didn't get to provide her with our loan. That's ok though because I know in my heart I was consistently kind, considerate and sincere and I not only did my job to the best of my ability but I did it with love. I know everything happens for a reason and that I didn't get that loan because GOD didn't want me and her to have it. I even thanked GOD for that experience because it gave me the opportunity to challenge myself with the golden skills that I am to teach the world and I did it. Not only that; I got to write about it.

Getting back to driving home when you drive by the accident that caused the traffic jam; did you ever take the time to thank GOD that you are not the one causing the accident or in the accident. I do and you should too.

You are home now. You walk in the door of your shelter. You will not be in the cold, wet or too hot. You are blessed with a real home with protection. Did you ever take a moment to thank GOD for your home? I do all the time. In fact, I constantly thank GOD almost everyday for my beauty, my home, my job, my Marine, my friends, etc. HE actually has told me that I thank HIM too much and to teach others to appreciate what they have.

Some of you are single. You might have a dog or a cat. Are you grateful for them? Enjoy them because I just lost my cat and I miss him so much. I tell my dog, she is the best dog in the whole wide world. I thank GOD for her all the time. I wonder why HE took my cat but I don't question HIM. I know there is a method to HIS work.

Ok, so you are single. It's up to you how you want to go about this stage of your life. I think we were meant to be with a partner so maybe you should work on that. Guess what, the chance of someone knocking on your door and falling in love is slim to none. You might be in a discovery time for yourself and don't want people around and that's ok too. If you're not, do something. Go help someone. Find something to do. Just don't sit there and watch tv. Read *Face Your Fears and Do It Anyway* and go meet people.

ToastMasters is an excellent way to meet people. You can be alone in your grave. Again this golden book cannot cover the scope of how to meet people but reading this paragraph might help a few single people realize that they need to work at finding the love of their life. I dated thirty seven men, read 400 profiles on <u>love@aol.com</u> before I found my Marine.

**Work hard at what you want
and you will get it.
You just have to really want it.
Build it and they will come!**

Those of you who do have partners; do you greet your significant other, your children and others when you come home. We have a love rule in our relationship. Kiss hello and kiss goodbye. It let's the other person know that we are home or leaving or we are mad at each other. My Marine used to not like it but now if he drives off and forgets to kiss me goodbye, he will actually drive back and find me.

Greeting and letting your loved ones know you are leaving for a while says I love you without actually saying those words. It also shows them and GOD that you are thankful to have them in your life as well.

Now there is work to be done. Kids homework, listening to how your kids day went in school, cooking, laundry, chores, etc. If you just follow THE GOLDEN RULE and do everything with love, everything gets done eventually. Make sure everyone gets a hug, a quick kiss, or at least an appreciated message to show that you are glad they helped. Sometimes it might feel like a chore but it really bonds the relationship. Just be a sport and try it.

It's dinner time. If you can, eat at a table with the household for at least three meals a week. If conversation is limited; go around the table with everyone for highs and lows of the day. Have you ever heard of highs and lows? It is so fun. Just ask every person at the table what was the best thing that happened to them today. Then ask, what was the worst thing that happened to them today? This is when everyone thinks and chats about the good and bad events of the day. We did this with our kids and it gets them to talk about stuff that is bothering them and what excited them. Again, just be a sport and try it; even if it is just you and your partner. It's a wonderful conversation starter and many times you don't even finish with highs and lows. Then again, sometimes we stay at the table hours after eating. Furthermore, it's great when you can brag about how you practiced THE GOLDEN RULE and how you Paid it Forward. It not only bonds relationships but it's great to see that your partner and kids really do care. It's like show and tell but it's about yourself and not an object. Just try it, everyone will enjoy it because everyone loves to be recognized.

PLEASE BE SURE YOU
KISS ME GOODNIGHT

One of my fondest memories was when I told my parents goodnight. I would find them somewhere in the house and kiss them gently on the cheek. Well, I have tried to continue this with my family and close friends. It just shows that I care enough to show them that I appreciate them in my life. Some are quite surprised but very much enjoy it. My Marine, he likes it so much he has started to do it to me. He used to sneak away without saying goodnight and without my kiss but he liked that I did it and now he usually does it to. That is a great example of THE GOLDEN RULE. You might give it a try. It's so loving and fun.

Just curious, have you ever thanked the people that raised you. Raising you took a lot of their time, didn't it? Have you ever told your mother or father or grandmother or whoever fed you in the morning and/or at night that you appreciated the spaghetti you cooked for me. Have you ever called or looked up that teacher or coach that made a positive difference in your life. I know the feeling is incredible, it is priceless when you get a phone call or someone announces at the family reunion that they appreciated that you picked them up after school so they wouldn't have to walk, or that you made sure they brushed their teeth and disciplined them with love.

My nephew really made my day when he introduced me to his wife. "This is Aunty Mary, she practically raised me. She was like my second mom. She was always taking care of my a**." He said smirking. Wow, that was such a remarkable compliment. I didn't even think he would have remembered. I was elated to hear that.

Your parents or whoever helped raise you deserves praise. As you praise your parents, you praise GOD. Besides they had to put up with you every day. Some children thank their parents all the time. I want to reach the ones that haven't. I wrote my Mom for Mother's Day and my Dad for Father's Day a card that listed as many things I was thankful for and each task they performed; back, middle and side of the card. They shed a tear or two when they read it. I felt so good about writing it. Try it, you'll like it. Don't be lazy. You only have one life and guess what, it is almost over. No matter how old you are. Do it soon because they might not be around much longer. Just think how they will feel.

Loved! Isn't that what we all want? What a way to show it. It takes less than an hour to do and the reward is such an incredible feeling.

Sure you can be thankful that you have a wife or husband, girlfriend, boyfriend, mother, father, son, daughter, grandparents, in-laws, dear friend that puts up with you etc. But do you TRULY **feel** grateful that these people are in your life. Just a quick note, I say "be" thankful and "feel" grateful to express a point of awareness. To be thankful is ho-hum thankful but to truly feel grateful is a deeper feeling of wow, I am so fortunate to have this, that or them. Do you see the difference? This concept is HUGE to grasp. This to me is living with passion. So don't just say you are thankful. Really try to feel you are thankful. Sit back and look at what you have and want what you have; that is experiencing gratefulness.

You will know when you truly feel grateful because it is an incredible feeling. GOD is teaching me to appreciate not only the material things I own but also to be grateful for who I am and love others the way they need to be loved. I am so lucky, blessed, fortunate and grateful that I have the best teacher in the world. I hope you allow HIM to teach you through this golden book.

When you reach knowing that you are truly grateful; you will want to treat the ones you love with love and respect. You will love them for who they are. No matter if you don't always agree with them. What We are trying to say here is if you tell someone you love them then treat them with love and practice THE GOLDEN RULE. NEVER raise your voice at them, ever again. Period! I don't know a single person on this earth that enjoys being yelled at, do you? Do the opposite; thank them for being who they are. Now that is being The Better Person.

To Summarize:

- Be thankful for what you have. If you are not yet truly thankful then do some of the exercises in this chapter.
- If you really are truly thankful you will thank GOD until HE tells you not to thank HIM anymore; it happens to me daily.
- Live now. YOU CAN SLEEP WHEN YOU ARE DEAD
- Don't be half-ass thankful; be truly grateful. When you are, you will feel the difference.
- Thanking GOD is praying to HIM as well
- Don't just exist; find your purpose
- Even when you are angry or about to get angry; practice THE GOLDEN RULE
- If you are single, get a life. Make it happen because nobody is going to make it happen for you
- Highs and lows at dinner
- Kiss good-night
- Thank the people who raised you. When you praise them, you praise GOD
- Don't be lazy; your life is almost over
- Never raise your voice. NOBODY likes to get yelled at EVER
- Realize gratefullnes.

CHAPTER 4

LOVE VS FEAR

It is such a coincidence that when I was a child that I used to cut out the Love Is . . . . cartoons. No it isn't; it was GOD'S plan the whole time. WOW! Remember this:

Although I loved love at a very young age, I didn't understand what love was until an ex-boyfriend showed me a definition that made sense. In Dr. Wayne Dyer's book, *Your Erroneous Zones*, is this definition:

"The ability and willingness to allow those that you care for to be what they choose for themselves, without any insistence that they satisfy you"

Once I read Dr. Dyer's suggested meaning; I worked on getting rid of my annoying habit of trying to change the ones I said I loved. I put this on my wall and read it daily until I finally accepted everyone for who they are. To this day when I am frustrated because I didn't get my way; I would go back to read it. Once I did accept everyone just the way they are, my journey veered to the right.

Even after reading and studying love, I still didn't know what love truly is. I knew how to give, how to share, how to be kind most of the time, but I was mean and ugly when things didn't go the way I wanted them too. Unfortunately I was very mean to the ones I loved. At that time, I didn't know any other way but I knew love wasn't supposed to hurt as much as it did. So I studied love. I realized although I loved love and loved the idea of being in love. I didn't know how to truly love because I discovered that I lived in fear.

Of course there are so many different meanings and ways to explain love and to express love but Our mission here is to share with you what GOD wants us to know about love. We will call it GOD'S LOVE.. GOD'S LOVE is expressed through THE GOLDEN RULE and doing everything with love. GOD'S LOVE is expressed with consistent kindness, consideration of everyone and being truly sincere. GOD'S LOVE is about being The Better Person. I know I am being redundant but again repetitiveness is how people learn. We want it to sink in until it comes naturally.

Living in GOD'S LOVE is having TOTAL FAITH. Once you have TOTAL FAITH, you will automatically live

Success is:

1) knowing who you really are + being proud of it!

2) Spending each day doing what you really s/ be doing based on who you really are

3) Doing so w/ JOY + LOVE, so that those that come in contact w/ you feel the effects of your fulfillment

It's funny because when I met my Marine, I was getting ready and he came to give me a kiss hello and saw all the stuff written on my closet door and I thought he thought I was a basket case. I was a little embarrassed but for some reason, I didn't care and I was proud of my growth; those affirmations got me through my divorce, helped me as a single mom and created who I am today. This is one of my favorites:

Below is a wonderful poem Audrey Hepburn wrote when asked to share her "beauty tips." It was read at her funeral years later.

For **attractive lips**, speak words of kindness...

For **lovely eyes**, seek out the good in people.

For **a slim figure</ U>**, share your food with the hungry.

For **beautiful hair**, let a child run his/her fingers through it once a day.

For **poise**, walk with the knowledge that you never walk alone...

People, even more than things, have to be restored, renewed, revived, reclaimed, and redeemed; never throw out anyone.

Remember, if you ever need a helping hand, you will find one at the end of each of your arms. As you grow older, you will discover that you have two hands; one for helping yourself, and the other for helping others.

If you have low self-esteem and are not confident; you are probably shy and missing out on living life to the fullest. Only you can change that if you want to. My ex-husband, bless his heart, tried many years to help me with my low self-esteem and confidence issues but I had to figure out on my own that these were my issues and I was the only one that could find the answer. I just wish it didn't take me so long. May We suggest you make time and figure out how you can become The Better Person with love and your confidence will follow. I worked extremely hard to gain what other professional women have. Again, I found it in books, tapes, and talking to people and then I met Anne at Toastmasters.

See how I kept challenging myself. If you are struggling with self-esteem go to a Toastmasters meeting and push yourself. Anne told me about how she struggled with breast cancer and repeated her mantra:

"Through Christ all things are possible."

Dah, it comes back to TOTAL FAITH. Again, another light bulb went off. You see, I didn't always have TOTAL FAITH. But now that I do WOW; my life is fabulous. I couldn't ask for a better life than what I have today. You definitely have to work at it. Build it and they will come. Force yourself.

At one time I was so afraid that I would stay in the house so I wouldn't have to talk to people because I was so concerned that I would say something stupid and nobody was really interested in what I had to say. I had agoraphobic issues. It took years for me to believe in myself. Nobody made me feel that way; I just felt I didn't fit in with people. However, today, I know why I was the way I was. It was

GOD'S plan for me. I had to take that journey and read all those books and discover who I am so I could write this golden book.

Finally, at fifty-something, I love myself and everyone around me. I am no longer easily intimidated, I will no longer allow people to take advantage of me, and I am not only allowed to have my opinion; I value it. Yet I must practice THE GOLDEN RULE daily with love. My mantra: do everything with love eliminates most of my bad attitudes when I am hurting. I finally realize that not everyone is going to like me but I also know it is their loss because I am a wonderful woman. I have forgiven anyone I needed to forgive so I could live a more peaceful life. I have learned to let go and let GOD take the junk out of my life. Now that is self-esteem. FINALLY! YIPPIE! I also realize I have many challenges to come but I know from experience that if I have TOTAL FAITH, believing everything happens for a reason and I continue to be consistently be kind, consider and sincere to others with love; I know that I will be able to continue with my peaceful, happy and content life in this greedy, confused unloving world.

Want what I have? Read this golden book over and over and over; do what We suggest and you will feel IT too. Live in GOD'S LOVE, not fear.

Did you know most of us speak to our family members and closest friends harsher than we do to our acquaintances? Think about it. We do this because we live in fear, not love. For example, I woke up with a smile on my face and excited about the day. My husband just asked me to do something for him that I think he does better than me. I didn't want too but I knew it was good for me. I was living in fear again. Snapping at him, see how fear takes over, I breathed loudly and heavy and bark out, "whatever"; meaning ok. Now if we had just met or I was talking to my boss, I know I would have had a different tone of voice and a different attitude. It's strange, I love my husband more than I care about an acquaintance or my boss but yet I have a lousy tone for him and a gentle tone for others.

Something is just not right. Wouldn't you agree? When you live in GOD'S LOVE, you just won't speak to anyone, especially the love of your life, with a condescending tone. If you do then you will realize that it was not kind and you will apologize and make it up to them. Once you practice living with GOD'S LOVE you will automatically have a pleasing tone or you will catch yourself. It takes practice and it is fun to challenge yourself on your tough days. You will be rewarded because your relationship will grow with more love. Wouldn't that be nice?

Obviously in the example above, I was not being The Better Person because I was answering out of fear. BUT I realized how I reacted to him and recognized I wasn't practicing THE GOLDEN RULE. See, I am still learning. Sometimes I am challenged hourly, but I recognize that my attitude stinks and that I have to work at being CKCS. Isn't it odd that we actually have to work at being kind?

Take a moment please and think about the way you speak to your husband, wife, boyfriend, girlfriend, children or family members. These are the people who you love the most, aren't they? Why would you treat them with unkind words or an unnecessary mean tone in your voice? We all do it, don't you? Ask them if the tone you talk to them is ok by them. Ask them to make you aware of the way you are speaking to them. Does it bother them? Some of my family members snap back and forth. They are used to it and that is the way they communicate. I'm very sensitive; I wouldn't ever want to become familiar to that method of interaction. You might even have to walk on eggshells.

Hmm. Walking on eggshells, what does that mean? Is that such a bad thing? Many people don't like that they have to walk on eggshells around the ones they love. The old saying has somewhat of an adverse connotation to it, doesn't it? It's almost like someone else is in control if you have to walk on eggshells. We don't like people being in control of us. Many say, I don't want to have to walk on eggshells every time I am around this person. Why should I have to watch what I say? It is my house or I am the boss or I am the wife, husband. Many couples say, we should be able to say anything to each other. Many people don't like to watch what they say and they just speak their mind. But should that be ok if you are going to hurt someone's feelings or make them angry. One of my-in-laws once said, "that's too much work and I don't want to walk on eggshells?" This person has hurt many without even blinking an eye. Too much work to become aware of your voice tones and the words you use to express yourself. Too much work to be kind. That's an aaaaah . . . come on, Ellen Degeneres. That is sad, isn't it? For those of you that are unconsciously kind; you are blessed. However most of us have to work at it.

If you do have to work at it, ask yourself if you are up for the challenge to be CKCS. I hope you are because the state this world is in; we need to have a change of heart. Everyone likes to be treated with CKCS. Nobody likes to be snared at, yelled at, spoken down to, not listen to or even told straight. There is a different way of saying everything, isn't there? Find a way that you know will not hurt the other person. Even if you have to think before you speak. Like telling someone close to you, they shouldn't have done something when they already know they shouldn't have. Is it really necessary to rub it in their face? Instead of telling them they were wrong, tell them that at the time they did what they knew how, just learn from it. We all make mistakes; it's ok. Even share with them a similar mistake that you made. For some reason it makes us feel better about ourselves when someone else makes the same mistake. We all have similar needs. We are all so different and we have different needs but do you know one single human being that enjoys being around a mean person. Don't you enjoy being treated with kindness, consideration and sincerity? Isn't that the way you want to be treated? Absolutely! Thus, don't you think others want the same as you? Absolutely! So what if you have to watch what you say. Not everything that comes out of your mouth is nice is it? Well, it should be. One of my customers told me:

You can always think what you want but you can't always say it.

If you don't agree, put this golden book back on the shelf and/or recycle it please. You are definitely not ready to read this golden book.

It really isn't necessary to say certain things in a mean way, is it? Like yesterday, my Marine and I were supposed to go riding on our Road King around noon. It was a beautiful day in mid winter and I was so excited about our ride. He got the bike out and washed it. I was doing our taxes and noticed it was getting toward noon. I went upstairs to change and notice shortly thereafter the bike was gone. He normally rides it after he washes it. It was now one o'clock and he wasn't back. I boringly sat and watched TV, with ants in my pants. I hate to call him unless it is important. I don't ever like to nag. I called and jokingly said, "where you stay?" (we talk like that in Hawaii, it's fun) He was next door hanging out. He said he would be home in a few minutes. Now in the past, that could be hours but he knew, or at least I thought he knew, how badly I wanted to ride. Well, sure enough he did come home and tells me that our neighbor is on his way over to visit. I told him in a bitchy tone, I thought we were going to ride. We will, he said. Well again, he took too long and I got frustrated and left. I always have a back up plan because I have learned throughout our marriage he doesn't always do what he says he is going to. That's who he is and I have accepted it. Others may not but I have. I was mad and I didn't kiss him good-bye because he disrespected me, to a degree. As I was driving, I went through the 7 Golden Steps To Solve Your Negative Junk as mentioned in the next chapter. He never said we were going to go at a certain time. Around noon could be 2:00pm. We weren't specific. So I really have no reason to waste my day being angry. I must admit it took me an hour or so to get over it. But I stayed focus at being ok with not riding even when I saw bikes drive right by me. As I drove up the drive way, GOD told me, "JUST BE KIND AND LET IT GO. HE TOO DIDN'T GO RIDING SO JUST LET IT GO AND ENJOY THE REST OF YOUR EVENING." This time, I listened and that is exactly what I did.

The really sad part is that it is actually easier to be mean, than it is to be kind.

Now, I could have and have in the past gone off on him and told him how inconsiderate he was and continued nagging but he knew he was wrong. I kindly told him to just let me know next time so I could make other plans and that was the end of it. I didn't need to make him feel worse than he already did. I will tell you though it took me to stay very focused on just love him than to tell him what I was thinking. Is that walking on egg shells? So what, he's happy, I'm happy and we had a great evening. GOD told me:

JUST BECAUSE HE HURT ME, DOESN'T MEAN I HAVE TO HURT HIM.

Now that is The Better Person, wouldn't you agree? Some of you won't agree because that was inconsiderate of him but I carefully choose my battles. I stand up for the ones that hurt my heart. I don't waste time on petty things like the above example. I could tell with this situation; it didn't stab my heart or make me sick to my stomach. It just made me mad. This has happened in the past, I solved this minor issue by not waiting for him like I used to. I have a life and I can find something to do without him. The faster you learn to pick your real battles and have a back up plan, the faster you can live a more peaceful, happy and content life like I do.

In the past before I did everything with love, I would probably still be mad this morning. I know we wouldn't have sat at our beautiful dinner table eating yummy left-overs, while enjoying the glorious sunset. I know we wouldn't have said grace and thanked the LORD for all that HE shares with us and asked HIM to keep us humble. We wouldn't have enjoyed the Pro-Bowl like we did that night and we wouldn't have kissed each other good-night. I am so glad I got over it. I'll walk on eggshell anytime. It's just better this way, wouldn't you agree? That is the huge difference of living in love and not fear. Are you living in fear or love?

Take a few minutes if you would and just think about how you treated your loved ones today, yesterday, or last week. Right now, this moment, I am giving you the opportunity to start a new chapter in your life and have a change of heart. Make a decision and a true commitment, a contract with yourself and GOD that you will do your best to practice THE GOLDEN RULE in every situation. You will do your best to speak with kindness in your heart to especially the ones you love. In fact, let's take this a step further and let's make a pledge to your-self and GOD that you will no longer live in fear because you will choose to do everything with love.

I, _____, will do my utmost best to practice THE GOLDEN RULE every day, even to those I do not enjoy being around. I will focus on being consistently kind, considerate and sincere to every person who I have contact with. I will diligently do everything with love. This is my pledge to myself and GOD.

Signed

_____

Love truly means that you never, ever hurt the ones you love or yourself. Does that make sense to you? Ponder on this please for a moment. Each of us, too often, don't think twice about how we speak to our loved ones, do we? You love this person, these people. If you love them then what gives you the right to speak to them so harshly or to give them the silent treatment or to slam a door or to cop an attitude. Because all these actions hurt the ones we love, don't they? We just get too comfortable, don't we?

**Living in GOD'S LOVE means that you
never want to ever hurt that person,
EVER!**

When my husband talks down to me, which doesn't
happen often, I often times catch him and say in a quiet
tone, "you are way too comfortable". That is one of our
clues when one of us needs to change our tone. Or I make
the sound of a horse. Meaning you need to get off your high
horse.

Often times, it is ok to speak in a different tone as long
as you know that it doesn't bother or hurt the other person.
Some families are rougher than others. I am not suggesting
you talk so politely like the two gophers, Mac and Tosh, in
the cartoon; but they are so cute. Some of you might

remember this cartoon. If you don't, please google it. Again,
it seems strange that this is one of my favorite cartoons. It is
amazing that GOD had HIS EYES on me when I was a
child. My point is, sure we don't have to go from one
extreme to the other. Like being mean to obnoxiously polite.
All We are asking you to do is to talk to the ones you love
and the entire population for that matter, as you would like
to be spoken to. It just makes sense.

Remember too of course, everyone's tone is different. I
like a sweet tone like most women do but that isn't always
the case with my Marine. So I am pleased with a kind
macho tone. It took me getting used to his tone after our
courtship. However, if he says something I really don't like

in a too harsh tone, I tell him straight but not in a bitchy tone. Honey, "did you need to say it to me like that. I didn't like it; that hurt me. How would you like it if I spoke to you like that"? Or if he acts like he knows it all; I gently remind him GOD wants us to stay humble and we are to help others do the same. He gets it and so will others in your life if you set the example. The sooner you do; the happier, more peaceful and content life you will enjoy.

Let me give you an example of staying humble. Like I mentioned earlier, we are in sales and we are so blessed to be very successful people at our job because we do our best daily, we diligently try to do everything with love and work very long hours. Well, with our success came boasting because we are so proud. However, GOD has mentioned to me several times. STAY HUMBLE. STAY OFF YOUR HIGH HORSE.

Sometimes that is hard to do when you are doing so well. Well, we didn't stay humble and started boasting to others about our success and it bit us. We went from being the top sales reps to the bottom ones. GOD humbled us big time. We deserved it. Just recently a new rep started with our company. He too went to the top but was so cocky that he would sit back in his chair like he owned the company and boasted, not taught, others how to do the job. Guess what, he didn't do so well the next two weeks. We have a weekly meeting and while we were having a tough week another rep was doing well. We walked into our meeting room with our heads down but not low enough to see a co-worker with her legs up on the table like she owned the company. My husband and I smile gently at each other. Guess how she did the following week? If we don't stay humble, GOD will humble us.

Thus we remind our selves constantly; our success isn't for ourselves, it is for you. So we can share with you what GOD has taught us. Doing everything with love is working for us and I was instructed to write about our everyday life to show that we too have ordinary lives just like you do and you too can have a more happy, peaceful and content life. You will as well, if you follow THE GOLDEN RULE (**CKCS**) and do everything with love. You truly cannot fail but you won't understand what I am talking about until you actually practice THE GOLDEN RULE every day.

I also want to share a humorous way my hubby and I have of dealing with each other when we say something jokingly hurtful or a wrong tone. If he or I say something derogatory in a somewhat kidding way, the person who said the silly statement has to get up and walk across the room and kiss the other on the cheek. An example of this is that we are close to the same height and we like to joke around a lot about little bitty people. The other day he asked me what my little pea brain was thinking. I told him this master mind is coming up with all kinds of incredible ideas for him and made the motion of tapping my finger on my cheek for him to walk across the room and kiss me right there. He laughed and did so. It is funny and fun. Remember you must teach the one you're with how you need and want to be treated. More on this in my next book, Be the Better Partner.

As you can see, it is not easy to be The Better Person. My Marine says, "being The Better Person is harder when someone else isn't." Isn't that the truth?

Just because the person you are talking with is living in fear, doesn't mean you have to live in fear with them.

This says that someone has to actually step up to be The Better Person no matter how crappy you are being treated. Thus you must always respond with calm words with a composed tone. You might have to breathe, pause, or quietly sigh before you speak; especially if someone is putting you down, unnecessarily criticizing you or just being mean to be mean. Our first reaction is bark back just as loud and quickly at the person that hurt us, isn't it?

Picture this if you would. Two family members are in the kitchen not liking what each other said and voices begin to get louder. One raises their voice and then the other reacts. Ugly words are being exchanged. It gets louder and louder. Now try this. As it gets louder, you, step up to be The Better Person, you lower your voice because you made the pledge to GOD and yourself to practice THE GOLDEN RULE. You don't like it when people raise their voice so you choose not to. At that moment, it might help you to repeat the mantra, "I am The Better Person", I am The Better Person". While the other person continues on a rage, you refuse to raise your voice and entertain this method of communicating because you want, really want, peace in you life. You remain composed, with an everyday, calm voice. You become the calming device. Sooner or later, after a few mean, loud, words are thrown at you, they too will lower their voice because they will look and feel pretty lame if they continue to yell. Thus you have taken control of yourself and if this family member loves you, they too will see that it was unnecessary to continue the exchange with raised voices. This might take a few times but when you maintain a composed manner, speak from the love in your heart and stay calm; you will both be in a better position to talk things out with love.

Now when I am in a situation that someone I love said something that offended me and I know the words out of my mouth are going to be ugly; I say excuse me, I need a time out to gather my thoughts. My Marine doesn't always like that I escape him because I just expressed my anger and flee. That isn't right either because it doesn't give him a chance to defend himself. Most of the time, I wait for him to rebuttal and then I politely excuse myself and leave the room quietly. Notice I said quietly. This is important because I used to leave the room slamming doors. I wouldn't throw things but if I was washing dishes; I would generate loud noises, slamming them. Currently, instead of slamming, I gently put down whatever I am doing and leave the room. My next goal is to be able to talk calmly about the problem and discuss the situation right then and there but I am not there yet. I still get too defensive and say mean things so I just take a time out. However, as I write and rewrite this golden book, I am improving daily because this golden book reminds me to do everything with love. So, keep this golden book handy when you need it.

Which reminds me, the other day I was in a bad mood and when I spoke to my girlfriend. I told her I needed to read my own golden book. She knew what I meant too. She could hear it in my voice that I was having a bad day. It's great to have a friend that will listen to you even when you are grumpy, isn't it? Thanks TJ. Well, after I hung up the phone I did read a couple of chapters. I forced myself to do everything with love and I felt so much better so did those around me. It really does work.

Composed calmness is a golden skill that will lead you to peace of mind. Awareness is first. You must admit that this is happening in your home first. I see it every day. The other day a Veteran called his wife and asked her if she found the paperwork we needed. She said she looked for it and couldn't find it. He went off on her and told her that she was supposed to find it and that the reason she couldn't find it was because she was so disorganized and that she never does what he asks. His tone was condescending and hurtful. She hung up on him. He was unnecessarily rude to her. How would he like it if she said that to him about his tools? He obviously was not practicing THE GOLDEN RULE. My Marine wouldn't speak to me like that because he wouldn't want me to speak to him that way. It is totally unnecessary to talk to anyone like that. Wouldn't it have been a more peaceful conversation if he said this instead:

> Hi hon, the loan rep is here and we need the paperwork that I asked you to find. Did you find it?

> I looked for it and couldn't find it.

> Ok, pause (because you are disappointed) well, where do you think it might be?

> I am really not sure.

> Ok, where do you think you would have put it and I will look for it. This is important babe that we find it. Try to think for a minute; where do you keep our important papers?

> I looked for it today Frank and I ran out of time.

Ok, but let's work on finding it because we
need them so we can save some money. I
am going to reschedule this appointment
and we need to find it together. Ok. Gotta
run bye.

Another sad incident, just recently, I was in a home
and a child kept coming out to see me and his parents. The
mother said "Get out of here you idiot"; "can't you see we
are busy."

Nobody is an idiot. Not a human on this earth wants
to be called an idiot; especially a child. Parents do this all
the time. They might not come right out and call their kids
names but when a parent says, you don't have a clue, how
can you be so dumb, or you are stupid if you think that.
These are all very harsh words and pointless. Sure, discipline
is necessary but there is no reason to be patronizing.

Ok, so now you are wise enough to admit that you
actually have been pretty mean to your family members.
What now, we always talk to each other like that. Well,
again, it is just a choice. If it is not hurting anyone, you all
agree then go for it. However, wouldn't it be a more peaceful
household if you all vowed to be kind to one-another. Start
by announcing this golden book. Tell your family or loved
ones that you want more peace in your life and that you
want to try some of the methods suggested in this golden
book that you recently picked up.

You don't need to apologize if you are hard headed but
start by saying good-morning. Sincerely ask them about
their upcoming day. If they do one thing nice for you or
your home; sometimes you have to look for it. Thank them,
tell them I appreciate that you _____. That is all you have
to say. Again:

I appreciate that you cleaned the kitchen.
I appreciate that you took the trash out.
I appreciate that you let me sleep.
Thanks for making coffee this morning.

Any words of appreciation tell your family member or people you live with, that you love them without saying the words, I love you. Sure it sounds funny at first but it sure is nice to hear. Don't you like to hear it when someone recognized what you did for them and not what you didn't do? Like when you cleaned the entire house for four hours but forgot to do the laundry. No one says a word about how great the house looks then someone has the audacity asks, did you wash my socks?

If you practice calm composure you will not go off. You will breathe and say something like, "ouch" I would have liked you to have told me how nice the house looked and you appreciated that I worked so hard today. Then ask, by any chance did you get around to washing my socks. Oh, that's ok, I will get them right after dinner. It's no big deal. Or honey, would you mind throwing them in the wash while I finish working.

There are so many different ways to say things. Even add humor and romance to a simple question, so that the family laughs.

So, did my bride of many hands have an extra one granted to her by the GODs of the vacuum to wash my socks?

Yes, your highness, pronounced your anus, in a playful loving tone, "in fact that hand got sucked up and I just couldn't get it back.

Make it fun. Especially chores around the house that no one, repeat no one enjoys. Or you could just continue quarrelling the way you currently do with the ones you love. It's just a choice, isn't it?

Keep in mind, while doing everything with love, don't ever let anyone take advantage of you or disrespect you in any sort of the way. Again, doing everything with love doesn't mean you allow someone to use you, take advantage of you or you have to be a kiss ass. There are times when you will get hurt but these golden skills will not only keep you calmer but you will also be so proud that you handled it with love. Your life will change because you will be much happier with yourself. You won't become immobilized all day or all week. The best part is, you can continue your daily life and not get wrapped up in such negative energy because you are in control. Which brings me to my next chapter; how I process solving my problems.

To Summarize:

- Dr. Wayne Dyer's suggested definition of love "The ability and willingness to allow those that you care for to be what they choose for themselves, without any insistence that they satisfy you."
- Demonstrate GOD'S LOVE by being The Better Person. When you have TOTAL FAITH, GOD'S LOVE will come automatic
- Are you living in fear or love?
- Force yourself to grow to be confident; only you can change. Do whatever it takes to attain self-esteem
- Want what I have, read this golden book over again until you get it
- How are you speaking to the ones you love? Do you have to work at being kind. Don't get too comfortable with the ones you love.
- Discuss a tone that is appropriate for your family
- So what if you have to walk on eggshells
- Have a change of heart
- Did you sign the contract with GOD?
- STAY HUMBLE
- When they get louder you get quieter
- Practice the golden skill of composed calmness
- Just because they live in fear doesn't mean you have to.
- Kind assertiveness is when you practice THE GOLDEN RULE but yet don't let anyone take advantage of you.

CHAPTER 5

7 GOLDEN STEPS TO SOLVE YOUR NEGATIVE JUNK

This chapter is another example of how I did everything with love and didn't fail. It took me a while but I handled it the way GOD wanted me to. This is the way I process negative junk in my life and this process will help you resolve your daily problems. By applying these 7 Golden Steps, your life will be more peaceful and much happier than it is now. This example happened while I wrote this chapter. A coincidence, nope; it happened just exactly the way it was supposed to.

Being redundant but making a point. If you truly believe and tell yourself over and over again that everything happens for a reason, your negative junk will be easier to accept and handle. It's hard to go through tough times but echoing my mantra will get you through anything:

If you work hard, have TOTAL FAITH
do your best, practice THE GOLDEN RULE
don't sit on a pity potty,
jump back up when you are pushed down
and you do everything with love,
your life will be grand.

Again, TOTAL FAITH will alleviate your stress. I know because when I don't have TOTAL FAITH and I have negative junk going on; I am stressed. I feel weak, frustrated, defeated, and get sick often. Like I have mentioned before, I haven't been sick in years because I do have TOTAL FAITH; even though I have negative issues in my life just like you do. Your life will change if you do what We are asking you to do. Truly knowing and believing you are part of GOD'S PLAN is such an uplifting enlightening feeling. Wouldn't it be nice to have peace of mind every day and to be happy and content even during the difficult times?

With that said again, getting back to my example. Something big time hurt me today. The moment I found out I was literally sick to my stomach. It is twelve hours later and I am still hurting and my body feels horrible. It is 4:00am. I cannot sleep. I wish I could throw it up and it would all go away. It won't so now I need to go to work on myself.

<u>I need to process it.</u> Let me tell you briefly what happened. This is hard for me to do but GOD told me to write this so that you can see how to settle issues with HIS LOVE and how hard it is for some of us to do but so worth it. This problem of mine might be petty to some but it really bothered me. It is just an example so that you can apply the 7 Golden Steps and it is happening now so I can remember it.

My Marine is friends with his ex-wife and there is too much detail to discern what is considered right or wrong. They used to speak on the phone often. I have a hard time admitting it but I don't like it when he talks to her about things other than discussions about their kids. Sometimes she would call at very special moments; like when I was buying my car, when we were on vacation or just when we were laughing and having a good time. Don't get me wrong, she is a wonderful person and a great mother to their children. I just didn't like it when they talk more than necessary. I am not sure why it bothers me, it just does. I am female. I am his wife now and I want him all to myself. Call it selfish; but that is the way that I feel. I knew in the beginning that they were friends and if I was to be in his life, I would have to accept it. In the beginning I would accept anything because I was so crazy about this man. Now, all the children are of age and I don't understand why he has to continue to talk to her but I do want to understand. Yes, I truly want to understand and be The Better Person and get through this. As mentioned earlier, there is more to this than I care to share and that is why it is probably taking me so long to get over.

Yesterday I picked up his ringing phone and saw that it was his ex-wife but her name was different. I recognized the phone number. He answers my phone, I answer his. I am not a paranoid wife thinking that he is having an affair. We trust each other. I just help him answer his phone because his job is so demanding. You see, when he got his new phone I didn't see her name on his call list. Well, he had changed her name because he knows I don't like it when she calls. Unfortunately, I saw this and became livid.

Breathe Mary, breathe. He was chopping wood out back. The old Mary would have taken his phone to him and called him on it right then and there. I would have spoken to him in an ugly angry tone; probably yell at him as well. I probably would have bitched myself right out of our marriage. I would have marched upstairs and called my girlfriend.

Not this time. This time I am going to use the 7 Golden Steps to process this by myself. Not with anyone else. I don't need to talk to anyone right now. My girlfriend is sick of hearing about the same issue anyway. Are your family and/ or friends tired of hearing about your same issues that you haven't resolved?

I say to myself, I need to figure out a way, with love, to handle this or I will not be practicing what I preach. When I first found out, I felt betrayed. My heart felt like it sank into my stomach. I was temporarily devastated. However, knowing that this situation is only temporary was a huge step for me because in the past I would have thought of the worst things possible. I had to take many deep breaths to keep me from yelling at the person I allowed to hurt me.

When I get in a situation like this, I know the first words out of my mouth are ones I wished I never said. So, I literally press my lips firmly together because I know those words will not only hurt him but will also make me feel worse as well. **I have finally figured out that hurting my husband and me is not going to be conducive to solving our differences of opinions. In fact, it makes it worse.**

Besides, my goal for my marriage, since I have become The Better Person, is to solve issues with love, with as little pain to all those involved and love him the way he needs to be loved. Those that are having problems in their marriage; I suggest you read that paragraph again.

> Tangent: I got this in an email one day. I would like you to think about this story every time you say mean words to anyone.

NAILS IN THE FENCE

There once was a little boy who had a bad temper. His Father gave him a bag of nails and told him that every time he lost his temper, he must hammer a nail into the back of the fence. The first day the boy had driven 37 nails into the fence. Over the next few weeks, as he learned to control his anger, the number of nails hammered daily gradually dwindled down. He discovered it was easier to hold his temper than to drive those nails into the fence. Finally the day came when the boy didn't lose his temper at all. He told his father about it and the father suggested that the boy now pull out one nail for each day that he was able to hold his temper. The days passed and the young boy was finally able to tell his father that all the nails were gone. The father took his son by the hand and led him to the fence. He said, "You have done well, my son, but look at the holes in the fence. The fence will never be the same. When you say things in anger, they leave a scar just like this one. You can put a knife in a man and draw it out. It won't matter how many times you say I'm sorry, the wound is still there."

author unknown
http://blessingsforlife.com/favforwards/nails

How many nails are in your fence? How many holes are in your fence? Thus, the best thing for me to do when I first get hurt or angry is to remove myself from the vicinity of the ones involved because I know I will probably have to put a nail in my fence. At this particular time I quietly go to my room and pace to burn off some anger. I didn't slam the door. How could I have been so stupid to think that he got rid of her phone number? I guess I expected him to cease contact with her since the kids are of age.

In a very emotional state of mind I first get angry, upset, frustrated and cry. Then I ask, ok GOD, what now, I thought that issue was pau (this means finished in Hawaiian; HE understands all languages). "JUST LOVE HIM" HE

say very few words to him. I refuse to speak to him with a lousy and degrading tone. I still love him and I don't need to hurt him if he hurts me, is what GOD told me.

YOU DON'T NEED TO HURT THEM
JUST BECAUSE THEY HURT YOU

If you want to be The Better Person, you must understand and apply that statement with every situation, even painful conflicts. At the same time, I have to validate my feelings; take care of Mary first and try to understand each others perception of this issue. Without thinking about any other problems in the past but just to stay focused on <u>this</u> difference of opinion is a challenge. No laundry list allowed to be discussed in this marriage anymore. Although I still sometimes harp on the past a little; I do so on my own time, not during this particular quarrel. However, with the wisdom I have now, I know that it is crucial that we just get mad at the problem at hand, learn each others perceptions, and come to a compromise or agree to disagree; followed by a warm meaningful hug. Many times that is easier said than done. However, the more I work on focusing on the issue at hand, the more peaceful the discussion is.

Ok, so now I am surrounded by beauty. Still angry but with TOTAL FAITH realize that this situation is temporary and I just have to process it. Nobody is going to do this for me. Like I said earlier, it doesn't do any good to call my girlfriend or anyone else. I need to process this myself with love. I know I am repeating myself and the reason is because the first thing most of us do when we are hurting, is pick up the phone to call someone who will solve the problem for us. I want you to recognize that your problems are your problems and nobody else's. Call them after you have resolved the issue with love. When you do fix this issue with love, you will feel great and be so proud of yourself. GOD will want you to boast about it in a humble manner.

GOLDEN STEP 2:
STATE THE PROBLEM IN LESS
THAN A PARAGRAPH

Before I actually state the problem I want to mention that over the years of any relationship, uncomfortable conflicts occur. You will want your way and they will want theirs, right? Some people call it a fight; some call it a disagreement and others say it is just a difference of opinion. I used to fight, then disagreed and now, most of the time, it is just a difference of opinion. It's so much more peaceful to see conflict as a difference of opinion because then it is easier to agree to disagree and lovingly accept the other person's perception and their opinion of your perception. If you are still raising your voice and saying things you wished you had not; it is a fight. Keep reading and work on solving your negative issues until it becomes habit where you will react automatically with love. Fighting is not fun. If you are having disagreements, that's ok, as long as you are not raising your voice.

When you reach a more peaceful state of mind and truly understand that conflict in a relationship is usually just a healthy difference of opinion; it is so much easier and faster to solve the issue and move on to your happy, peaceful and content life. You will have less negative time and more positive loving time added to your life. What a concept. You will eventually be proud and able to Pay It Forward and help others. Also, don't forget to go to our website and tell your story on how you had a change of heart.

Getting back to Golden Step 2: State the Problem. When you state the problem make sure you don't include a different issue of what happened last week, last month or last year. I keep repeating myself because you must get in the habit of discussing with yourself and the others involved, only the incident that recently happened which made you angry or hurt you. Also, if you can't talk to the person over a period of time, whether it's a day, week or month; it would be kind if you would let them know that you need your space and that you still love them but need a time out.

Now that I have stayed with the current issue, I need to see the truth for what it really is. Not blaming anyone but myself. I take full responsibility for my feelings. I have always said to my kids, husbands and co-workers, let's not blame anyone; let's just fix the problem. Seeing the truth for what it really is, means; don't make it worse than it is or don't make it better than it is. Try to see what exactly happened which I will show you how to do that with the next golden step.

So, when you state the problem be as concise as you can and just talk about what just happened. Try to get to this golden step as soon as it happened because over time what you saw and heard gets distorted. State exactly what happened and how you are feeling in less than a paragraph. A paragraph is approximately three sentences. This is my statement for my example:

I don't like my husband and his ex-wife talking to each other about anything but their children. I am not sure how I feel; I just don't like it.

After you state the problem it is time to figure out what really happened.

GOLDEN STEP 3:
ANALYZE THE PROBLEM

Analyze the problem means identify exactly what happened and why. See it in their eyes as well as yours. In my younger unwise years I would blame everyone around me, thinking he doesn't care if I am hurt and I would stay angry for a ridiculous long time. At this age, I don't waste that time, I begin to process it as soon as possible. With seeing the truth for what it is; I first ask myself a bunch of questions:

- Is it really that bad?
- Am I making a big deal out of something that I should just let go?
- Does this really need to be discussed?
- Am I getting upset because I want to be in control of him/her?
- Sure I am hurt but why am I hurt?
- How am I going to resolve this issue again and for the last time?
- What would I do if I was in his/her shoes?
- How is he/she feeling right now?
- Do I really want to hurt him/her?
- Did I say something I should not have? Were my negative body language, tone, and actions necessary?
- Did I really do my best?
- I might say I practiced THE GOLDEN RULE but am I sure I did?
- Should I get off my high horse?
- Am I living in a state of fear or love?

It took me many stupid years to realize he doesn't do things to intentionally hurt me because he feels my pain as I feel his. If you really do love someone, don't you feel their pain as well? Not when you're mad you don't normally feel their pain because you are self absorbed and are living in fear not love, right? You feel your pain but not others, wouldn't you agree? Again, make sure you ask yourself what truly happened and why you are hurting. Most of the time, I will pathetically admit, I want to be in control of whoever hurts me. As I grow up, I don't need to be the boss as much in any given situation. I used to be impulsive, brash and bossy, now I am kind, considerate and sincere which has brought me more peace in this greedy, confused, unloving world. But right now I must continue to process this junk with love.

Analyze your negative issue so that you can see all three sides; your side, their side and the true side. My side is I don't want him talking to his ex-wife because I am self-fish and don't want to share him. It's not fun to see my husband laughing and enjoying her company. Yet I don't want him to feel guilty when he does. His side is he wants to remain friends with her so that he can continue a close relationship with his kids. She has control over this and he must abide by her rules or she will be given the opportunity to keep the children at a distance. I am not saying this is what she will do but why give her a reason to do so. The true side is really what is best for their children. I need to understand this. I need to accept what he feels is important to him and his children. He is not attracted to her and so I know there is not going to be an affair. I am not threatened by her in any way. Call it jealous, I am not sure what it is. I haven't figured it out. It stinks and if I don't get over it; I will hurt our marriage. So I turned it over to my exceptionally intelligent teacher, GOD. My wonderful husband is a really good man. He is an extremely friendly guy. He cares about everyone. He helps everyone. She is a good person and wants the best for their kids as well. They aren't hurting me intentionally. I am hurting myself with my self-fish immature and insecure feelings. My Marine has many friends that love him because he is such a great guy. I truly do not want him to feel bad or guilty when he is having conversations with her.

Before I solve this ongoing negative junk in my life, I would like to elaborate on seeing the truth for what it is. Every human being has their own perception on how they see things. The following is an example how people have different perception.

The other day I was with a friend and she was telling me how she felt deceived by a phone conversation with her mother-in-law and husband. While talking with her she expressed the bossy tone she used when she talks to these family members. I let her know that her tone sounded condescending and asked her if she thought it was necessary to communicate with the people you love with that tone. She didn't realize her tone was bad until I mentioned it.

She told me they were going on vacation; their annual family reunion. Of course there may be more to this story that I am aware of but this is what I got from what she shared with me. She grumbled that her mother in law wanted her to stay in a hotel close by. Unfortunately, my friend had made reservations in a hotel in advance and it was far from her mother in law. My friend was quite upset that she is the one that has to change her reservation to move closer to them. She wanted complete control of the situation and wanted her mother-in law to change her reservation. There was no monetary loss and she would lose nothing but pride. However, her mother-in-law and husband would be 'in control" if she was the one to change her reservation. Like most women, my friend likes to be in control of her husband. Sure she enjoyed the people and service at the far away hotel but I asked her if she enjoyed her mother in law. She said yes.

This is where I see things different. From my perspective I saw that her mother in law wanted her to vacation near-by, instead of miles away. To me, if she enjoyed her mother in law's company then it is a compliment that her mother in law wants for her to stay closer. So what if she has to change her reservations. She will be The Better Person if she bends a little and lets go of being the boss.

Hmm, she replied and the next day she tried Our method, to do everything with love. She called to cancel the hotel far away and is now going to vacation in close proximity of her mother-in-law where they will be able to enjoy each other's company. She's had a change of heart. She is happy, her husband is pleased that it didn't become an argument and her mother in law is excited. Win, win for all. Do everything with love and you cannot fail. Again just try it. She really enjoyed that she too can produce a loving spirit within and share it with others.

If you've not had the pleasure of a loving spirit, please try some of the teachings in this golden book and you will not want to go back to the old you. Having a loving spirit is indescribable and We really want you to experience it.

So how can I resolve this difference of opinion with validating my feelings while at the same time, validating his? Yes, both feelings must be validated. You must try to understand where the other person is coming from. Wouldn't you like for someone else to validate your feelings. Well, they would like you to validate theirs. Doesn't that make sense? That is an example of practicing THE GOLDEN RULE.

You could come up with your own list of questions. I am not going to answer the above questions because I need to reserve some of my personal life. However, I found that to solve this ongoing issue for the last time means I need to realize most importantly that my feelings are controlled by fear, not love. If I was living in love there would be no negative issue in this situation. I vowed to GOD that I would have TOTAL FAITH and do my best to do everything with love. You see, I am so dedicated and blessed (please notice I didn't say lucky; this isn't luck, this is GOD'S BLESSING), that my INNER VOICE reminds me constantly by asking me if I was living in fear or HIS LOVE. You on the other hand will probably have to work on your relationship with GOD to get to where I am at. Just practice what We have talked about in this golden book and talk to HIM every day and HE will visit you. HE told me to tell you that you can have a relationship with HIM, if you want it. Don't forget to have TOTAL FAITH because HE answers those that make an effort. I know because recently HE spoke to my Marine.

Feeling embarrassed in front of GOD, I now realize my anger is unnecessary because I really should be pleased that in the last year my Marine has diligently worked at validating my feelings. He tries very hard to stay loyal to me and I should see that it is inconvenient for him to talk to her outside of our home but he does. He is bending and so must I. I must appreciate that he has not ignored how I feel. If I think about it, he continues to be kind, considerate and sincere.

Sometimes thinking about the goodness of the one you are mad at, is difficult to do especially when you are in the heat of the moment but you wouldn't have them in your life if they were bad people, would you? So after you calm down think about how they do not want to intentionally hurt you. Sure they want their way as much as you want yours but they don't want to see you hurt; unless you are frequently a mean person. Remember mean people suck. So get it in your thick head that he or she doesn't want to hurt you; they want their way, so what, unless it is harmful to you or others. Most of the time, it is just a difference of opinion. Just remember the person who cheerfully bends more, is more likely to have more peace of mind. Doesn't that make sense?

Thus, I need to bend too and truly accept their friendship.

GOLDEN STEP 4:
BEND AND ACCEPT WITH COMPROMISE.

To accept their friendship I have to <u>truly</u> accept it this time and just enjoy that he has one more person that loves him because he is such a great guy. Yes I said enjoy because if I don't truly enjoy seeing that he has one more friend, I will continue to hurt myself. I convinced myself that I am done hurting with this issue. I don't want her to be angry with him because he doesn't want enemies and I know he hates conflict. I wouldn't want that because I truly love my husband. It would be easier for me to have him all to myself but it wouldn't be for him and his children.

Again, I tell myself, I want to live from love not fear. I have a change of heart. I feel this wave of peaceful relief as I tell myself kind, considerate and sincere thoughts. Sure I have to bend and so did he. Isn't that what marriage or any relationship that you want to strengthen must do. He has validated and respected my feelings by speaking to her less and less. Changing her name so I don't see it on his phone was done not because he didn't want me to see who was calling but it was because he saw that it hurt me when she did. It's imperative for me to hear and see his perception and for him to hear and see mine. He actually has been keen on my perception and I was ignoring his; because of my stubbornness. I wanted things my selfish way. I wanted to be the boss who is in control. He rarely answers and keeps his conversations limited when he is in front of me. He keeps trying and so will I. I cannot wait to call my girlfriend and tell her that I had a change of heart.

Now, that is living in love, not fear. Wouldn't you agree? How about you; are you having negative, painful conflicts in your life that need to be processed? What is bothering you? What keeps you from having peace of mind? What or who makes and/or keeps you angry or sad? Is it your husband, wife, partner, brother, sister, mother, father, mother in law, father in law, brother or sister in law, cousin, co-worker at work or you? What is keeping you from living with love and why are you staying in fear? Do you have control issues? Do you need to process the negative junk in your life? If so, try these 7 Golden Steps and ideas.

Now that I have seen the truth for what it really is, while not blaming anyone but myself, and having analyzed and solved the issue at hand, by bending and accepting, it's time to go home with love. In the past this has been very difficult because I didn't know what to expect. I was living in fear and would hope he wasn't home when I got back so that I could have more time for myself. Often times it would take days to get over; where we wouldn't speak to each other. I finally learned the best way to handle these differences of opinions.

It took me years to realize he would react to my actions. I think most people are like that. I have found that if I act with love then he will react with love. If I walk into our house still angry and mad, he will be angry and mad too. However, if I walk in to our home with love and kindness, he reacts with love most of the time. Sometimes we stay angry but if he sees that I am consistently calm then he will also remain calm.

As I walk through the door my heart is thumping not from fear but from love. This is brave of me to do this with love; yet it feels good. Think about it, after you have argued with the ones you love and stepped away to have a time out. Isn't it tough to face that person again no matter who you think was wrong? That is why most of the time it is easier and makes sense to let go completely of blaming anyone and just fix the problem at hand. It truly is best to stop focusing on "they did this to me" because in all actuality you allowed them to do that to you. We say you may have to bend more than the other but when they see you predominantly bending; they too will eventually bend for you. Sure it might take time but as long as you love this person and they are not physically or mentally abusing you and you still enjoy each other, then isn't it worth the time to humbly teach them THE GOLDEN RULE?

Once I am in the door we usually start off with an under the breath, hi. I usually break the ice with small talk about the cat, dog, sports or weather. Then we gradually make our way to pleasant every day conversation. Subsequent to those interactions I suggest we talk and discuss each other's perception. I am the one to initiate the perception discussion. This is when we sit in a room together, often at the dining room table for serious issues and the living room for discussion that need to be brought out but not as troublesome.

Every so often both of us are not quite ready to discuss anything just yet. Anger is still in the air. You know the feeling. Well, take more time then because there is really no sense in talking just yet. Talking to an angry person is like talking to a drunk. It's better to be patient and give each other enough time to process their anger. As you practice these golden skills; it should take less time to process. After trial and error of practicing these 7 Golden Steps you will be proud of yourself because you will have less negative time and more positive time. Once you experience what that means, you will love life more than you ever have before.

However, you might have to bend more often than they do. If you both read this golden book and if you truly love each other then you both will want to bend. You will also see how it is harder to be The Better Person when someone else isn't. It is a challenge and some of you promised GOD to try to consistently practice THE GOLDEN RULE. Not only am I pleasing GOD but I have more peace after the argument and that allows me to enjoy my life just a little more.

Now we are ready to discuss our differences. At that moment, I ask his perception of what happened. I will elaborate on these questions in my next book: Be The Better Partner. Here are a few questions to ask and make sure you listen without interrupting. Take notes if you have to but let them say what is on their mind.

- In a calm, gentle tone ask, do you know why I was angry, hurt, mad, sad, etc?
- Can you understand why I was feeling this way?
- How did you see it?

- What was your perception of what happened?
- Did you see it my way at all?

A discussion is with both people not just one sided, right? Both speak in a quiet civil tone because remember you love each other. When he/she tells you how he/she saw what happened different from what you saw; you need to accept that he/she actually perceived it that way and it isn't even close to how you were thinking. Sometimes it is shocking to hear how they saw it and vice versa. After you have your turn to describe what happened through your eyes, then ask, did you see it my way at all? At that time hopefully, you will both be kind, considerate and sincere and say yes, I can actually see it the way you do or I now see why you were so upset with me. If I saw it that way I too would be upset. Once we do recognize why were angry we make sure everyone has had a chance to verbalize their opinion.

Now, it is time to continue on with what we were doing for the day; getting on with enjoying our day. At that time the discussion is pau (finished). No more needs to be said about it. It doesn't have to go on for hours. In fact, I like when my Marine says, why are we still talking about this? Or I thought we were done with that issue.

It's time for a hug and a smile. He gives me both and asks if I am ok. Actually I am, I reply while looking up to GOD with a smile. I realize this might not be the end of this issue but it is no longer ugly because I have truly had a change of heart. I said that twice because it is not easy to truly have a change of heart but when you do, oh happy day. As long as I truly accept it is ok for him to be friends with his ex; I will be at peace with myself and both of them. He actually deserves to enjoy another friend that cares about him. I can embrace the thought and follow through with kind, considerate and sincere actions. WOW, what a great feeling! It no longer bothers me when I see her new name on his phone because I think how wonderful my Marine was to try to protect me from getting hurt. I actually embrace this thought every time she calls. Wow! That was worth me taking the time and 7 Golden Steps to process and solve this negative junk.

A few weeks later, my Marine flabbergasted me. We were listening to music as we often do and he told me he wanted to play this song when we renew our vows. I was elated when he entertained me with Tracy Byrd's, "Keeper of the Stars" and then blew me away with Tanya Tucker's "Strong Enough to Bend"

> There's a tree out in the backyard
> That never has been broken by the wind
> And the reason its still standing
> It was strong enough to bend
>
> For years, we have stayed together
> As lovers and as friends
> What we have will last forever
> If we're strong enough to bend
>
> When you say something that you can't take
>   back
> Big wind blows and you hear a little crack
> When you say "Hey well I might be wrong"
> You can sway with the wind till the storm is
>   gone
> Sway with the wind till the storm is gone

Like a tree out in the backyard
That never has been broken by the wind
Our love will last forever
If we're strong enough to bend

When you start thinkin' that you know it all
Big wind blows and a branch will fall
When you say "Hey this job takes two"
We can sway with the wind till the skies turn
blue
Sway with the wind till the skies turn blue

Like a tree out in the backyard
That never has been broken by the wind
Our love will last forever if we're strong enough
to bend
Our love will last forever if we're strong enough
to bend

www.cowboylyrics.com

What a prize that was when he asked me to dance in our living room. I fell in love all over again with my husband. It was worth bending and accepting. I think I will bend whenever I can.

Unfortunately, during your transition to be The Better Person, there will be times where there will be no compromise. That is when you should, agree to disagree. It is extremely rare when people agree on every situation and that is ok. With some issues, no one in the relationship is willing to bend or find the middle ground. However, if you live in GOD'S LOVE, not in fear, you will bend. When I was living in fear, I didn't always compromise but I did agree to disagree and go about my day. Living that way is not as happy and definitely not as peaceful as living in GOD'S LOVE but it worked and I forced myself to be ok with it. Now I don't have to force myself to be happy, it is automatic because I know if I do my best with love and have TOTAL FAITH, I will live a more happy, peaceful and content life in this greedy, confused and unloving world.

Moving right along, solving your problems usually entails forgiving someone, including yourself.

GOLDEN STEP 5:
DO NOT JUDGE
FORGIVE YOURSELF and OTHERS

As I process any issue, I find Golden Step 5 the toughest golden step and often I judge easily and by-pass forgiving. It really is too easy to go about your daily life hastily judging others, isn't it? We do it all the time. I say I don't but I do. Again, I am not a saint. One of the Veteran's I helped yesterday caught me when we were talking about my golden book. I mentioned the example I gave earlier about the woman who had all the church décor and was on her way to church but was unkind to me. He was right. I did judge her. I also judged my Marine's ex-wife without realizing it. This is something I am still working on and I really cannot elaborate as much as I would like to because I still judge people inadvertently. However, now that I have the golden skills to be The Better Person; I don't judge as often. By the way, judging is negative. Complimenting is always okay. Stating a fact is also not judging. Learning the difference is the challenge.

I was actually going to take Do Not Judge Others out of this golden step but GOD told me not to delete it. I used to not always do what my INNER VOICE asked of me but now I do. So if this part sounded incomplete it is because HE told me to just be aware how often we judge people when we should leave that to HIM.

Obviously, all people are not the way we want them to be. There are a lot of unfortunate and some mean people out there but we don't know what their life is like. We don't know what they have been through. GOD asks that we feel for them, yet, don't judge them. HE is not suggesting you feel sorry for them and pity them but HE would like to enlighten you with the feeling of compassion. This I have and do daily. When I see a homeless person on the street; I first see that I am so fortunate to have what I have. I give what I can even when I don't have much to give. I will even do a U-turn if I have time. I know that person is there for a reason and just be thankful for my life. I don't feel sorry for him. I show him compassion by sharing my gift of money or food. I don't judge them, don't tell them to get a job, or try to decide if he is faking his poverty. To me, if he or she is on the street making $300 a day; they are there for a reason. Maybe it was GOD showing you how fortunate you are. I smile at them hoping for a smile back. I don't care if they are capable of getting a job. It is not my business. I don't know why they are in the position they are in; I don't need to know. I do know, GOD wanted me to see them; not to judge them but to share my love with them.

When I am dealing with someone who is angry or mean; I shower them with compassion. I give them no reason to be mean to me. Sometimes it takes a while and you will need patience to wait for them to return this kindness but it is so worth it. Look at it as you are teaching them THE GOLDEN RULE. The reward is usually just a smile. I hope that is enough for you. Most of the time, it is for me. Then again, sometimes there is no reward. However, as long as you know you did your best with love, then you will have more peace of mind. Mission accomplished.

Now that I have accomplished being compassionate, I can continue to work on forgiving those that I allowed to hurt me. If you don't follow through with this golden step, it is most likely that the same issue will occur again, and again.

For some time now I have had another large issue that was causing anxiety in my life and while I was processing the problem above my sister in law came to visit and we were sitting in my front yard discussing the negative junk in our lives. She profoundly stated that the only way she is going to get over what she was going through was to forgive herself and the person that she has allowed to hurt her. Then the light bulb went off. She's right! She gets credit for bringing real peace back into my life.

I have been wrestling with a negative event for over a year and I have to forgive myself and the people that I allowed to hurt me in order for me to have peace again. I wish it wouldn't take so long for light bulbs to show me the light. Ok, so I must process this some more. Truly getting over your anger takes time and is worth it because you don't have to waste more time on it later. It is sort of like an investment into your life. If you spend this much time now, you will reap the benefit later.

Finally no more tears over this issue because I have worked through the 7 Golden Steps and I think I have completed Golden Step 5: Do Not Judge and Forgive Yourself and Others; only time will tell. It took me a little too long to forgive them because my stubbornness kept me angry and ugly.

However, GOD told me that the only way I will have the peace of mind I had experienced before the ugly event, was to truly forgive all people involved and just to let go and let HIM handle it. I think I have. FINALLY! WOW! What a wonderful feeling! It has taken over a year to let go and let GOD but I think I have finally solved this issue as well.

You will know when you truly forgive the people involved because when you hear their name or see them in the future, you will be able to do so with a true compassionate smile and not a pretend fake one. Only the future will tell for me. I hope it is a real compassionate smile. If not then I have more work on this golden step.

GOLDEN STEP 6:
LET GO AND LET GOD

Let go and let GOD is another imperative step. To let go and let GOD is also the final golden step to actually solving your problem. When you have completed the six golden steps above and have attain the ability to control your thoughts and let go and let GOD; you will have a happier, peaceful life.

Throughout my growth and while I was in the process of constructing these 7 Golden Steps; I would find myself, like I mentioned earlier, immobilized and continuously harping on what had happened; wasting many hours, days and sometimes weeks thinking about the same negative junk. Thank goodness my girlfriend listened to me on a daily basis to help me figure out how to process my junk. The negative issue that I was trying to process would stay in my thoughts way too long and I often times could not get rid of it. Kind of like a song that you can't stop humming all day but these thoughts are not as fun as a song. So I have a couple of ways to force myself to stop thinking about negative junk.

If I could not solve my problem within a day or so, especially when I am in a situation where I know I either have to agree to disagree or leave the relationship, I would give myself only fifteen minutes of the next day to think about that issue and then after that time frame I no longer would allow myself to think about it again for the rest of that day. I would literally set the timer, whether it be my oven or my cell phone and when it buzzed I would say to myself and sometimes out loud; Time is up, that's it; give it to GOD. I would at that moment ask GOD to give me the strength to let go of this issue and go about my day with love. If it is still bothering me the next day; I again would set a timer and give myself another fifteen minutes to process and that was it. I would say STOP, take a breath and force a positive productive thought into my head. Sometimes I would yell STOP out loud and shake my head just to break all the destructive gibber jabber in my head. Once I discovered from Dr. Wayne Dyer that you can only have one thought in your head at a time; I eventually gained control over my thoughts. As silly as it sounds, I still have to tell myself that I can only have one thought in my head at a time and it might as well be a pleasant one. I had to:

STOP THINKING AND JUST LIVE

Thus, to let go and let GOD, is to block out the destructive talk in your head and ask GOD for the strength to get through the day. Do whatever it takes for you to limit the time you spend thinking about the negative junk in your life. You can set a time, a buzzard or have a friend call you to remind you to let go and let GOD. If you aren't into

GOD then give it to the universe. I plan to set something up on my website so that you will spend a limited time thinking about the negative stuff that keeps you down; an alarm of some sort. Maybe we will eventually have an apt for that. We suggest you do it for your peace of mind for that day. Don't think about tomorrow or the next day. Just stay focused on happy thoughts for that day.

As Scarlet said in *Gone with the Wind*, with her beautiful southern twang:
"I can't think about that right now. If I do, I'll go crazy. I'll think about that tomorrow."

Otherwise, you will not only waste the day but just think about the things you could have been doing. I didn't realize how much time I was wasting and you normally don't understand. That is when I remember what my daddy taught me,

TIME WILL HEAL ALL WOUNDS

When I realized my life is more than half over; that is when I started let go and let GOD more often. The faster you develop this golden skill; the more days you will have to enjoy your life.

Staying busy is the best way to keep your mind occupied with positive thoughts. If you are busy then you don't have time to think about things that are out of your control, do you? Do whatever it takes as soon as possible so that you do not allow yourself to linger on with issues that are probably out of your control. Joyfully move on. If you can't think of any positive thoughts or ways to keep busy, volunteer to help someone. It cost nothing to volunteer and the reward is priceless. Get off the couch, turn off the tv and go visit a child, a single mom, a disabled person, a senior or a family member who is lonely. When you focus on others you don't have time to feel sorry for yourself, does that make sense to you?

To reiterate, to let go and let GOD means to stop thinking about that negative junk and get on with other positive, productive thoughts. It's time to let go and let GOD when you can no longer do anything to make the situation better to your desire. As my Marine would say, this just in, you are not always going to get your way; live with it; adapt. As long as you know you did your best by following the 7 Golden Steps to solving the negative junk in your life and you practice THE GOLDEN RULE by being CKCS and you know in your heart you did everything with love; that's it, you have exhausted all means. Now it is time to let the rest go and let GOD take it from there. At that time you must let go of all thoughts pertaining to the subject in its entirety and force yourself to get busy. You have to admit to yourself and to GOD that you have done your best and that is all you can do. You have finally come to realize that the rest of this issue is out of my control. Breathe and make sure you thank GOD for all you do have and move on to Golden Step 7 with a big smile.

GOLDEN STEP 7:
EMBRACE THAT YOU WORKED HARD and HANDLED IT. NOW PRACTICE THE 7 GOLDEN STEPS IN EVERY NEGATIVE SITUATION UNTIL YOU CAN TRULY DO EVERYTHING WITH LOVE

Remember when I said, "Credit is due where credit is deserved". Now you get to pat yourself on the back and you get the credit for doing such a great job. You did your best with love and followed the 7 Golden Steps. Doesn't it feel great? It should if you were true to yourself and the others involved. You must reward yourself with acknowledgement that you are developing these golden skills, growing with love and on your way to being The Better Person. While you were applying the above 7 Golden Steps, you probably realized that it really is easier to be the mean, confrontational person. However, The Better Person is so much more fulfilled and enlightened. As you try to become The Better Person We want you to be in touch with how it feels. Does your mind feel lighter? Like a rock was taken out of your brain. I did work hard on these problems and I do deserve credit. My Marine sure did reward me with the songs, he gets credit to. Most important though is I followed through and continue to do so; no matter what the given situation. I am strong enough to bend and so are you. No wonder I now have such a happy, peaceful, and content life, do you?

Now if you are bending but still angry, hurt or resentful. Go back to Golden Step 1: Let Your Emotions Out and start over. Spend some more time; ask yourself more questions. Journalize if you want to. Write the words, do everything with love and you cannot fail on the top of every page to remind you to do everything with love. I wore a gold heart pin on my tough days and held it during the moments when I had to force myself to be kind, considerate and sincere. I was an angry person. Presently practicing THE GOLDEN RULE comes naturally. Invest more time in getting over your negative junk so that you don't have to deal with it again. Going around in a circle with the same issue is not fun. I did it for years and years. First, I would get mad and have a fight; then I would forgive the person even if they didn't apologize. I would actually put too much blame on myself. Then we would have great times. Then I would get angry again. It was a vicious cycle that got ugly. The faster you realize you are in this destructive circle of pain; the quicker you can get to work on it.

We hope it doesn't take you as long as it took me. It is such a remarkable lift in my heart when I decided to follow through with Golden Step 5. I am in the process of truly forgiving all involved and to love and accept and embrace all that happened. It is time to move forward and teach others how good it feels when they follow these 7 Golden Steps to deal with the negative junk in their life. Yes, I have had a change of heart and I feel GREAT. Now, I can joyfully move on to help others.

I am not of authority to tell you how to solve your problems but I know these 7 Golden Steps work for me and when you take a conscious effort to solve your problems with love, not fear, you will live a more peaceful, happy and content life. Once you master these 7 Golden Steps and begin to feel the peaceful surreal feeling; you will want to do it again and again. If fact you might even welcome conflict because you will know how to handle it. It truly is a remarkable feeling knowing that you can handle any negative issue that you will encounter in your journey of life. When you apply these 7 Golden Steps over and over again you will gain more confidence in yourself and love yourself more than you do right now. To be in love with yourself is a wonderful thing. Try it you will like it.

Unfortunately you will have days where you will forget about doing everything with love. Like yesterday, I slipped up but my INNER VOICE kept me in line by reminding me to be kind and let go of my petty anger but I was stubborn and I didn't for a few wasteful hours. In the past

I would harp on these minor inconveniences for days. I've gotten so much better at letting things go.

I went to court yesterday for a speeding ticket and I was only sometimes kind, considerate and sincere. I was inconsistent. As you know, my goal is to be consistently kind, considerate and sincere. I had such a difficult time doing so 100% of the time but I did learn from it and will try to be consistent next time. I realized after talking with my Marine, I wanted to, once again, be in control. When I got the ticket, I was so upset that the Trooper wouldn't take me back to where he tagged me. He was in control and I wanted to be the boss. He was doing his job and I realized I don't need to tell him how to do his job. I should have at that time just paid the ticket and be done with it and moved on peacefully; but nope, I was going to show him when I got to court.

So today in the courtroom, I blamed the Trooper for not being able to read the ticket with all the scratch marks and I concocted many other excuses but got nowhere. When I went to pay for my ticket, I attempted to make the whole system ugly when I blamed the people in the office, the trooper and the judge. I detest court but I was wrong for acting the way I acted. I didn't make a scene but I could have been more affable. When I started to judge the people in the office, GOD said not to. There was a woman who was goofing off while she had a line of people, who were also getting inpatient. I did hold my tongue because my INNER VOICE told me, THEY PUT UP WITH OBNOXIOUS PEOPLE ALL DAY, FIVE DAYS A WEEK; LET THEM HAVE A LITTLE FUN. ISN'T IT NICE TO SEE PEOPLE LAUGHING. Somewhat frustrated, I let it go and left. At that time, I should have smiled and looked up to thank HIM and be grateful that this is the only bad thing in my life right now; but I didn't. I went to my car and called my Marine to get the sympathy I was looking for in the courthouse. I didn't get it from him either; he did as GOD did and reminded me to let it go and come home and enjoy the rest of our day. I didn't listen to him either; I called my girlfriend. I am glad she didn't answer. I needed to get over this insignificant junk myself. However, after a fabulous fried chicken dinner which my wonderful Marine prepared for me and a glass of wine; I finally let it go. I am proud of myself because the old angry Mary would have written a nasty complaint letter to the office staff and letter to the Trooper. That would take up more negative time and I wouldn't have the peaceful positive feeling I have right now. Instead of writing the letter I enjoyed the Celtics basketball game and got up this morning to share with you how I am still learning. Wanting to be in control; kept me from appreciating the rest of my day and most of my evening. Lesson learned; don't let my mind get bogged down with petty stuff. Move on quickly to productive, fun thoughts. Hopefully there won't be a next time, but when there is, I will do my best to handle the event with consistent kindness, consideration and sincerity.

Are there issues in your life that keeps coming up, over and over again keeping you from having peace in your home? Do you handle situations outside the home with love or do you treat strangers as if you want to be in control of them. When you start practicing these 7 Golden Steps for solving your negative junk, you will experience the peace of mind that I am so fortunate to enjoy. We want that so much for you, whoever you are.

It's fun, fulfilling, rewarding and exciting to be The Better Person. The other day I was inadvertently rewarded. I was at an American Legion Auxiliary meeting and we were going over the details for a fashion show we had planned. Flyers and tickets were already printed and I had recently informed the organization that we were donating the proceeds to them. Well the building we were going to use was already booked for that day and we had a problem. Now with my golden skills of practicing THE GOLDEN RULE and doing everything with love; I knew nobody wanted to be blamed. I stayed calm and smile and said proudly, it's ok, I live by this philosophy, let's not blame anyone; let's just fix the problem. An elderly, wise and classy woman next to me said, "I like that. That is a good philosophy." So we did. The president had a tear in her eye but we worked together with love and resolved the problem. We get to use the building, it was a win, win for all; on with the show with love. No one was hurt and we all felt good during the process. While we were repairing the problem; the president looks up at me as I laugh gently and the adjutant says, "what?" The president giggles slightly and said "oh, it's just Mary, she is always so kind and happy." What a reward that was and MISSION ACCOMPLISHED.

To Summarize:

- Let the 7 Golden Steps be your guide to help you solve your negative junk.
- **Golden Step 1:**
  LET YOUR EMOTIONS OUT
  o **Happy Spot**
- **Golden Step 2:**
  STATE THE PROBLEM IN ONE SENTENCE
- **Golden Step 3:**
  ANAYLZE THE PROBLEM
  o **See the Truth for what it is**
  o **Don't blame anyone**
  o **Ask a bunch of questions**
  o **Perception**
- **Golden Step 4:**
  BEND & ACCEPT WITH COMPROMISE
  o **Agree to Disagree**
- **Golden Step 5:**
  DON'T JUDGE & FORGIVE YOURSELF & OTHERS
- **Golden Step 6:**
  LET GO & LET GOD
- **Golden Step 7:**
  EMBRACE IT, PRACTICE UNTIL ITS A HABIT
  o **EMBRACE THAT YOU WORKED HARD and HANDLED IT. NOW PRACTICE THE 7 GOLDEN STEPS IN EVERY NEGATIVE SITUATION UNTIL YOU CAN TRULY DO EVERYTHING WITH LOVE AND IT BECOMES HABIT**

CHAPTER 6

I'M HAVING A BAD DAY

The other day I was having a really bad moody day. When was the last time you had a bad day? Let's go back to it and analyze it for a moment. Was it a somewhat bad day where a few things didn't go right or was it a really bad day where you felt grumpy all day and just couldn't kick the bad mood you were in?

My struggle with mood swings lasted for years, intermittently. Thank you GOD for teaching me how to minimize them. During these mentally painful mood swings, I would blame my ex-husband, kids and my Marine. They alleged that I would twist their words to create an argument. Often times I was a mean person and like I have stated throughout this golden book:

MEAN PEOPLE SUCK

When I had my mood swings, it was like the boogie man (the devil) would get into my head. Well, one day, my Marine didn't tolerate my crankiness like he usually did and told me to go unf^#* myself. That was not nice but it woke me up. He was right. Over the years, my loved ones were reacting to my words, actions and tones. I didn't want to continue to be that mean moody person to him or others with my lightning tongue, especially after I received the email about the nails in the fence.

Are you a mean moody person? I had enough of my meanness. I so desired to be The Better Person. So I went to work on Mary. Do you need to work on you? Do you inadvertently make things worse than they really are? That's a tough one to admit. Once you can confess that <u>you</u> are the cause of your unhappiness; you could be on your way to being The Better Person. I made things worse but didn't realize it. I needed a time-out to find a way to rekindle that loving spirit I once had. The one my Marine fell in love with.

Just curious, have you ever experienced a loving spirit? I bet you had it when you were courting with someone. Take a moment and please think about what you were like when you were courting, dating and falling in love. You were not only kind, considerate and sincere but you also did many activities and met your partners needs with passion, didn't you? Who was the lucky person? Think seriously for a moment about the tone you used when you spoke to each other when you first met. Think about how you would drop anything you were doing if you could help this person. Think about how most of us would be careful to say things in a nice way. Even when you were angry, having your first disagreement, remember how you would lovingly do your best to mitigate the intensity of the argument.

GOD and I are not asking you to always be courting everyone you meet but please work on having this loving spirit by practicing THE GOLDEN RULE all the time and you will become The Better Person by habit. What a nice habit to have; don't you agree? I say yes because I know it feels great. Try it you will like it but you must try.

Well, it was so worth the time to heal myself because I now have really bad moody days only once in long while. It's like I have been healed. I take that back. I have been healed. Because now when I have these bad moody days, I know what to do, how to snap out of them or how to handle them with love; GOD'S LOVE. Being healed is a wonderful feeling! Thank you GOD!

Here is an example of maintaining my loving spirit. Yesterday, both my Marine and I had appointments 75 miles away. His appointment wasn't home. He was in the same area that I was headed so I thought it would be a great idea if he would cover my appointment while I write. Well, he didn't want to. He wanted the rest of the day off. I had to drive 150 miles so that he could have the rest of the day off. I was not happy about that. I started to cop an attitude and I admit I was short with him on the phone; not mean like I used to be. I did my job and came home around 11pm, tired. I was a little grumpy with him but my INNER VOICE kept repeating, DO EVERYTHING WITH LOVE, DO EVERYTHING WITH LOVE. JUST LOVE HIM. DO EVERYTHING WITH LOVE, JUST LOVE HIM. HE WORKS HARD TOO.

I had to remind myself and empathize that he is required to work every day; seven days a week. I get plenty of days off and I was able to help a Veteran which gave me a nice pay check. I had a change of heart and kissed him. I got over it way quicker and I was able to bounce back to my loving spirit. How would you have handled that situation?

Getting back to that bad day in the beginning of this chapter; pardon the tangents. Just need to write them as they happen so you can recognize that disagreements with loved ones happen every second of our day. It is Our job to teach you how to handle them with love as soon as they occur. To live every second in love, not fear; is Our goal. The more you do everything with love; the more others will follow your loving footsteps.

Mood swings are horrible, aren't they? You feel miserable and so do those around you. Nobody deserves to have them but if you will look at mood swings as a teaching mechanism that will help you balance your inner self, you will soon be able to appreciate them. Yes, I said appreciate your bad mood.

First you must agree that mood swings are a form of temporary mental illness that can be treated and can heal just like a physical illness or wound. It's ok to have a physical wound, isn't it? Well, it is ok to have a mental wound too. Some people have physical illnesses, some have mental illnesses and some unfortunately have both. Mental and physical illness should be thought of and treated the same. Of course, all illnesses have different intensities but most illnesses and wounds are hopefully temporary. It's not worse to have a mental illness. Just like a physical wound or disorder, like a broken bone, if you don't get immediate attention it will get worse, won't it? You must attend to these abnormalities immediately or you will probably have to have surgery or lose a limb. You don't want to lose your head, do you?

You must get it out of your thoughts if you think it is worse to have a mental illness. You are not slow, dumb, retarded, stupid, lack courage or any other derogatory description when you struggle with controlling your mind. You have abnormalities just like everyone on this earth. There is not one person in our world that doesn't have some sort of an abnormality.

HAVING ABNORMALITIES IS NORMAL.

Our abnormalities make us different, stronger and help us grow. You must believe that for you to heal.

It took me years to understand, accept and embrace why I would say the dumbest things, take longer to learn a task, or to have to read things way more times than other people. I was always so embarrassed to be around people because I didn't like that those were <u>my</u> character flaws. These are a just a few of my abnormalities. I took responsibility for them and for years I worked on changing some and most I just accepted and now laugh about.

I was temporarily mentally ill when I was dealing with my mood swings, struggling with my identity and my anger issues. Millions of people, especially women like me, go through these emotional rollercoasters, especially during menopause. Are you one of them? Most of us are not to the intensity of having to be institutionalized but I definitely had serious issues with my anger habits, identity and mood swings. I must say though, I wished I knew how to isolate and work on myself with these golden skills before I hurt those around me when I was suffering from this pain. I wouldn't have as many holes in my fence.

What abnormalities can you admit to?

Which ones do you need to work on changing?

Which ones should you accept and embrace?

The hard part is to first admit to <u>your</u> abnormalities. Have you yet to understand, change, and/or accept and embrace these idiosyncrasies that make you different.

Serenity Prayer

**GOD grant me the serenity
to accept the things I cannot change;
courage to change the things I can;
and wisdom to know the difference**

Be proud that you are different!!!! There is only one of you and that is great!!!! What a phenomenon, you are the only one exactly like you. Thank you GOD! When you were growing up it was often times embarrassing to be yourself, wasn't it? It was probably because you were afraid of what people might think of you; you lived in fear. You still might be living in fear. I hope this golden book encourages you to try to live in love. Once you do live in love you will be pleased that GOD created you exactly the way you are. You will laugh out loud more often.

You will also hold your head up and smile while you pass by people when you start living in love.

Why is it that most of us look the other way or look down when we walk by people? Wouldn't it be better if we could just walk with our head looking at the passerby and smile? I know it isn't easy to do because I am working on that these days. Or better yet, why can't we look for something nice to say like, I hope you are having a good day. More on this subject will be discussed chapter 7. Again, just believe in Our concepts and try them out and you will live a happier, peaceful and content life in this greedy, confused, unloving world. Has it clicked yet?

When I was dealing with my mood swings and my identity, I would read and listen to tapes that guided me to accept and embrace my abnormalities. It took many decades of attentive reading to uncover the talents I have and to accept that I don't do some things as well as others can do them. One of my favorite things to say when I do something dumb or can't do something,

**"GOD gave me many talents but I don't
do that one very well."**

Once I could actually admit that it is ok not to be able to perform as well as others, I was so relieve and a very relaxing calming wave came through my body. It was finally ok if I wasn't as intelligent as other business women. It is ok that I cannot pronounce some words. It is ok that I have no upper body strength. It was ok that I am slow and have to have people repeat things or rewind the beginning of the movies I watch. I think I have ADD because I have difficulty doing two things at one time. Oh, well it's ok. I was never tested but I have to work two to three times harder than most people on certain things. However, I am extremely creative, loving, sincere, and my tenacity, persistence and organization skills are my qualities which are conducive to my success. What are your qualities? What things do you do well?

Above all, I know I have GOD in my life who has a plan for me. All I had to do was ask HIM and listen to HIS answer.

**Once I listen and committed to having
TOTAL FAITH, I accepted my
abnormalities with approval not shame.**

It took me decades to like myself. So, if you are struggling with things you don't like about yourself. First uncover what you are good at, gain confidence in those talents and then work on changing what you don't like about yourself. Finish with accepting and embracing what you cannot or don't want to change. I encourage you to do your homework on you. Seek out what you truly enjoy and that you are not doing something to please someone else. Take some time to find what you like to do before your life passes you by.

My mood swings were tied to my identity crisis; are yours? If you do have mood swings you know it is hard enough to deal with yourself when you are on this emotional rollercoaster, right? However, it makes our job of healing ourselves more difficult if people are nosey and negatively criticizing us, isn't it? Wouldn't you agree that it's not right how people talk stink or gossip when someone is struggling with mood swings and say in a condescending voice and tone, oh they take Prozac, Wellibutrin, Zoloft or some sort of anti-depressant, to help them function. Whereas, it is not gossip and not talked about in a humiliating manner when someone breaks a bone or is hurt in a car accident. Both are painful, both want something to help them get through their day, and both want to be healed, right? It is really sad that one gets positive compassionate attention and the other gets negative disdainful rejection. Please feel compassion for anyone in any kind of pain, especially our soldiers who are mentally and physically hurting.

> Tangent: My American Legion Auxiliary just sponsored a fashion show to contribute to an organization called, HIDDEN WOUNDS. This organization was founded when a Veteran

returned from war and was mentally distressed. He cried out for help and no one would listen. He was not physically wounded. He was mentally wounded and our society didn't give him the help he needed. Please be just as compassionate about a mentally wounded Veteran as you would a physically wound Veteran. Just recognizing that this wound is just as painful as any physical wound that our Veterans endured will mitigate the pain our Veterans suffer from. I predict this organization will be extremely successful because there are more mentally wounded than physically wounded Veterans. They both deserve the same attention, don't you agree? If so, please visit their website: http://hiddenwounds.org and please donate whatever you can.

It's time to change our society's thought process; mental pain is just as painful as physical pain. We need your help. Pain hurts; it all needs loving help period. Who are you or anyone to judge what that person is going and been through. Male or female, it doesn't matter. That person is hurting. Why does it matter why they are hurting. It is none of our business if they don't want to share. The fact is they are hurting. Ask yourself when you are gossiping negatively about someone who is taking an anti-depressant; does it make me feel good to say these things? I hear it all the time. If it does feel good or even ok, something is not right about you, wouldn't you agree? Read this again if you talk stink about others. That is probably you as well as everyone. Even I have to work at this still. My Marine, he doesn't talk stink about others. In fact, I don't think I have heard him say anything he can't say to their face. I want to get where he is; I am almost there.

When I find myself inadvertently saying something negative about someone I stop myself and say out loud, I shouldn't have said that. We want you to stop if you are destructively gossiping. Teach and force yourself to stop. Say <u>out loud</u> to the person you are chatting with at the time, I should not have said that; I really don't know what they are going through. I don't live with them. I have no right to talk like that. Please excuse me for saying that. I need to remember that I am so blessed that I don't have their issues. I need to stay focused on being The Better Person with my own issues. Take responsibility at that moment and be aware that you said something that could hurt someone. If you cannot say it to their face, DON'T SAY IT! KEEP YOUR MOUTH SHUT. You don't always have to be talking, do you? It's better to be silent than to talk bad about someone, isn't it?

If you have to talk and don't like silence then compliment that person you are about to say something bad about. Challenge yourself and force yourself to find something good about the one you are about to talk stink about. Or walk away and repeat, do everything with love. Do everything with love. Sometimes you have to say it until you actually handle the situation with love. Then you can smile, even laugh out loud and say, I did! You will feel so proud of yourself.

Once you learn this golden skill and master it you will love yourself more than you do right now. Loving yourself and all others is one of the secrets to happiness, ask GOD. It's only a choice, isn't it?

Who's in control of your mouth?

Use this as one of your sayings. Let's go over that again. It is crucial if you want to become The Better Person that you learn this golden skill. When you find yourself in a situation where you are about to say something bad; ask yourself first, can I say that to their face or in conversation with others while they are present. If you cannot, don't say it. There is really no reason to say it if it is going to involve hurting someone, is there? Hold your tongue and think about something nice to say about that person.

FOR GOD'S SAKE; JUST BE THE BETTER PERSON

Tell a story about what happened to you that week, talk about your or their hobbies. Better yet ask the person you are with, what do you do for fun?

Challenge yourself. Even if the person is a selfish negative mean person who constantly frowns and always wants their way.

Or remove yourself from this person's life. Change your thought process and teach them to live in love. Shower them with kindness and give them not a single reason to treat you disrespectfully. Show them how the feeling is remarkable when you can actually find something good in all people, even if they have hurt you or have not been kind to you. Once you learn how to always be kind you won't want to gossip about them because at that time you will be able to say to yourself, I am finally The Better Person and it feels great! Then you will be able to Pay It Forward.

You know you can't take back things you say but you can develop an awareness when you do talk about others. We all do it. We want to teach you.

IF YOU CAN'T SAY IT TO THEIR FACE THEN NEVER SAY IT

Realize and become consciously aware that you do say things in a gossiping manner to others and eventually if you consistently catch yourself you will stop. Again, for some this will be a challenging task. It happened just the other day. I am in the process of looking for a good skin care program. I was with one provider and the product worked very well and I shouldn't have changed but a friend of mind asked me to try what she was using and so I gave her representative my business. She was doing her presentation and sold me the product but after the presentation we were chatting about a retreat she went on and said something that was not necessary. She said something negative about one of the most famous skin care providers in the world; the one I was currently using and like. The meeting went so well until that moment. I politely said I don't think that is true and I don't think people should say things like that when they don't know for sure. Even if they do know; it isn't necessary to put down another company ever. In the beginning of the meeting I told her I was happy with this company and that they are a wonderful organization. She agreed and said she doesn't put down other companies. She did degrade this business with her statement but didn't realize what she was saying because she probably does it every day and thinks it is ok. IT'S NOT! She is a church going, kind person but does not live by THE GOLDEN RULE. She needs to ask herself; would she like it if someone said that about her.

This is what GOD wants to change. This is why We are writing this golden book. It is not necessary to gossip. It so ruined my meeting with her. She would have been better off saying nothing about the other company and continued to talk highly about hers, period.

Now I must admit that I came home and told my Marine and questioned myself about my gossip about her. Here's the difference I think, correct me if I am wrong. I am venting with my husband and he doesn't know her or her company. I talk to him about almost everything; especially if something is bothering me and this bothered me. If I was to mention this story again to another person, I will never mention the name of her or her company; like I did in this golden book. There is a fine line and the line comes in when you don't say their name. We all talk about people and that's ok but let's not mention their name unless it is positive and complimenting. I am tempted to tell my friend what I thought but I am The Better Person and I will only tell her what I thought of the product. I know this woman is close to my friend and I will respect and appreciate their friendship. Their truly is no reason to bring this up again. I vented to my Marine and with my golden skills, I don't have to keep talking about it. I also am so proud the way I spoke to the representative.

For those who gossip about you; have compassion for them because they are judging you. When they judge you, then they are not The Better Person, are they? It's best to stay away from people like that or shower them with kindness. I didn't say kill them with kindness because that indicates some anger. There is no reason to be angry with them because they are the ones who are unhappy with themselves. Empathy is the feeling you will eventually have for them. Obviously these people are hurting and you might give them this golden book so they too can find a little more peace. At this point I will let go and let GOD. I hope you agree with what I am saying here because if you do, you definitely are on your way to be The Better Person and the feeling is so enlightening.

Once you realize you are gossiping, catching yourself gets easier. Soon enough you will be able to take it to the next level with a compliment a day. More on complimenting in Chapter 7, Pay in Forward. Let's work on your mood swings before you can start handing out compliments.

Once you admit that you are mentally ill with mood swings, that sounds bad I know, but only if you let it, then it's time to get to work on you. Don't stay focused on how it sounds; just fix your-self. I said it that way and didn't change the wording because We want you to realize it is very serious to you and especially, to those around you. Not admitting that your mood swings are a mental illness will deter you from becoming The Better Person. You could, if you choose, to call it unhealthy but mentally ill designates urgency. We are all unhealthy but we don't usually do much about it. Calling mood swings, identity crisis and anger issues mentally ill has more impact which is in need for immediate intense attention. Does that make sense?

Just to throw in, me, personally, I would rather have a mental illness than a physical disability because I know I am in control of my mental illness. I cannot control a physical illness as well. After you admit to yourself that you are mentally ill and unhealthy then you need to convince yourself that asking for help when you have a problem with mood swings is sometimes necessary. Think of it as just part of your journey and work on it so you can soon help others work on their mental struggles.

These mood swings can be temporary if you work at it. They will happen less and less if you learn the golden skills in this golden book.

If you are unnecessarily angry, mean, or unkind, you are mentally ill.

Thus, you must wholeheartedly admit that you have mood swing, anger, and/or identity issues or any other abnormality that affects those around. Express to your family that you need their help by agreeing to give you the time you need to grow and heal. Once that mission is accomplished, then take a few minutes and sit back, breath and give yourself a pat on the back. You have just taken another huge step to a happier, peaceful, and content life in this greedy, confused and unloving world. Feel blessed and thankful that you have the capabilities to work on healing this annoying behavior just as someone can work on healing a broken bone.

Now, picture yourself getting up smiling and ready for a productive day to help others. You greet your family with a kiss on each person's cheek and say good-morning. I am so blessed to have you in my life.

When you decide to take control of your aggravating mood swings, be brave and courageously share with your loved ones that you are having a difficult time with <u>yourself.</u> The longer you take to admit full responsibility the longer it will take for you to heal and become The Better Person. Why wait if you know that you can have more peace in your life. Are you ready to have more peace in your life?

If you do want more peace in your life, then with drive and ambition force yourself to have TOTAL FAITH.

Sit your family and friends down together or individually and share your struggles with them. If they love you then they too will want you to heal so you can have more peace. Apologize for your past mean behavior and tell them that you don't even like yourself when you are suffering from this maddening temperament. Make a commitment to them that you will practice THE GOLDEN RULE. Show them your contract with GOD. From this moment on try your best to do everything with love while you push through this tough time. Get them to empathize with you even though you have been so mean to them. They might have been mean to you as well but remember people react to what you say and you react to what they say. Someone has to step up and want to be The Better Person and stop this vicious cycle. Don't you agree? Yes or no. When I was in therapy my counselor gave me this:

Stages of Recovery

Stage 1: One day I walk down the street. There is a deep hole in the sidewalk. I fall in.

Stage 2: The next day I walk down the same street. There is a deep hole in the sidewalk. I fall in again.

Stage 3: The following day I walk down the same street. There is a deep hole in the sidewalk. I see it is there. I fall in. I can't believe I did it again.

Stage 4: The day after that I walk down the same street. There is a deep hole in the sidewalk. Can you believe I actually fell in again?

Stage 5: Finally I walk down a different street.

Are you walking down the same street falling in the same hole? Now it is time to go to work. Don't listen to anyone but GOD and your inner voice when people gossip. Talk to GOD, ask HIM to give you strength to get you through this temporary discomfort.

Ok so how do you work on mood swings, identity crisis and angry out-burst. First and foremost, read this golden book over and over until it makes sense. Second, practice these golden skills on your family, neighbors and sales people. Do it until you feel different. Read other books, see Appendix. Take the time to work diligently on changing the things you want to and accepting things you cannot. Read the serenity prayer as your mantra. Display it in your bathroom. If you are struggling; put a copy in your purse or pocket. Write love on your hand. Wear the heart pin I discuss later in this chapter.

If you find that you are hurting others, get help. If you have to take medication to help you get through this time, take it. You don't have to take a pill for the rest of your life to be happy but for right now, maybe you need something. Don't stay stuck and miserable. So what if you need to take a pill for a little while to help you get through these temporary tough times.

DO NOT BE EMBARRASSED IF YOU HAVE TO TAKE A PILL TEMPORARILY TO HELP YOU BATTLE YOUR MOOD SWINGS

When I was going through the early stages of menopause, I was embarrassed, at first, to admit that I was mentally ill and that I took bupropion, an anti-depressant. It took me months before I admitted to myself that I was a drag to be around. My husband was so patient with me. I couldn't put my kind Marine through my pitiful mood swings. I went to a psychiatrist and I am so glad I did. You will be glad if you got help too. As I write this, someone I know is too proud to go to a doctor to get help and take something to mitigate their pain. This person is crying almost every day and hurting others. What kind of pride is there in hurting yourself and others? On the other hand, I was talking to a co-worker and she told me that she had to take Zoloft for almost a year because of her mood swings and identity crisis. Both have pride, one was just wiser.

I enjoyed my happy pill and so did my Marine. I found my loving spirit again and I no longer need the pill. At first, I didn't know how I would ever give it up but GOD made that decision for me. HE told me I wouldn't need it. With TOTAL FAITH, practicing THE GOLDEN RULE and doing everything with love, GOD told me I was ready to let go of it and didn't need to order another prescription. I stopped taking it. Of course, HE was right I am better without it.

However, when you make the decision to take an anti-depressant or as I called mine, a little happy pill; don't think about how you will get off of it. Just live one day at a time. Live your life with TOTAL FAITH, practice THE GOLDEN RULE, do everything with love and you will eventually want to give it up. You will know when you won't need it any more. It's ok to take something to help you get through these mood swings and other junk in your life. Go ahead try it, give it some time to work and if you don't like it then stop but at least try it. Tell yourself and those around you that you are doing it because you don't like the way you treat others. Those around you will appreciate you thinking of them. It normally takes a couple of weeks to work. Be patient, keep a journal of some sort; mark it on your calendar. When your loved ones see how it is promoting kind behavior and you are pleasant to be around, they will be serving you your happy pill with your favorite beverage. When they do, thank them and don't be insulted. Thank them for their patience too. If you cannot thank them then realize that is a sign that you are still healing. You must feel comfortable with taking something before you can stop. Does that make sense? Because once you admitted you really do need help, then you are closer to not needing help. It truly is ok to take a pill until you are healed just like you would take an anti-biotic if you had pneumonia.

In other words, you must admit you are sick before you can heal. Just like our friend; he dislikes going to the doctor. However, skin cancer is prevalent these days. He ignored the signs on a daily basis and it got worse. Finally he went to dermatologist and was diagnosed with skin cancer and went through the steps for healing. Don't ignore your symptoms: meanness, anger, unkindness. Get help before it festers and gets worse and you lose the ones you love because of your stubbornness.

Going back to the beginning of this chapter, my really bad day; I had so much to get done that day but I couldn't shake the junk in my head. Literally, when I am in this type of funk or harping on a problem that I know I have to let go and let GOD; I vigorously shake my head up and down, side to side to get the boogie man out of my head. It feels good for a moment but it doesn't scare always him away. The boogie man is here to temporarily stay for the day. Yuck! The shaking not only creates my awareness of my mood, but it reminds me that I will have to work on being happy for the day. As silly as that sounds, for years, I had to work on being happy. That day I had my work cut out for me. I force myself to be ok. I couldn't get to the happy feeling; ok would have to do.

As I analyze that challenging day; nothing unusual happened. I got up ok. I enjoyed my yummy hazelnut coffee with ice cream; thank you GOD and Miss Geneva. I did notice I was weak while I stretched early that morning. Not a single bad thing was going on in my life but for some reason I didn't greet my Marine with a good morning kiss. Something was just not right; I knew it was more than just an off day.

Like we all do, I have on days, off days, really good days and really bad ones. After many years of wondering why I was so irregular, I have finally become aware of my moods and physical abnormalities. That is Our goal here for you. Be aware of your moods and how they affect you and others you come in contact with.

I now not only accept but appreciate that I have productive and semi-productive days; normally it's every other day. For example if I am in full speed with joy and tons of love for everyone; being very productive; that is a good day. Nothing can stop me, especially when it is a full moon. Normally, the next day, I typically slow down a little to recharge my batteries. Many years subsequent to the discovery of my pattern, I not only was frustrated that I couldn't always be in a good mood but I battled with myself to do more than I could. Always pushing myself until my body and GOD told me otherwise.

We all know <u>nothing</u> is easy. Just think about it for a minute what it takes to make a phone call; one phone call can take hours, can't it? That is enough to frustrate anyone because we are so busy these days. Or a project that is supposed to last only a couple of hours, lasts days or sometimes weeks. Unfortunately, often times, our expectations are a set up for disappointment. We suggest that you don't create negative energy with these types of everyday endeavors. Getting frustrated or angry while you perform everyday chores, errands and activities is, if you think about it, is sweating the small stuff. In the past when I was always sweating the small stuff, my Marine would say,

In the grand scheme of things, what does it matter?

Light bulb went off; that was my mantra for years until it really sank in. In the grand scheme of things, what does it matter if my house was disarrayed for an extra day. In the grand scheme of things what does it matter if my Marine is an hour late or doesn't want to participate in an activity I want to do. Unless, of course I expressed to him specifically that I wanted him to be home for a special event. In the grand scheme of things, what does it matter if your kids don't set the table to your exact liking or the towels aren't folded the way you want them folded. Sure some things matter more than others but think about which ones are really important. If it is not mentally or physically hurting someone; in the grand scheme of things, it truly shouldn't matter. Do you find yourself sweating the small stuff? Think about it hard; in the grand scheme of things it is all small stuff.

> Tangent: Do you know that nobody but you and maybe your significant other cares about what you look like or your hair color, or that your shirt has a hole in it. Nobody cares about the color of your living room or the type of furniture you buy. Nobody cares but you what kind of car you drive or the color of your outfit. We do care if your zipper is down. That is always

a little uncomfortable for everyone. However, nobody really cares if you added 5 pounds of weight. What others only care about is how you treat them and if you sincerely care about them. If they do gossip about it, they need this golden book. We are building a lanai (patio) and my Marine would say, when people come over they will like our addition. It really doesn't matter what they think; it only matters what we like. When we showed a family member our newly painted living room; his comment was; what color was it before. He doesn't and shouldn't have to remember. Sure it is nice that our friends and family enjoy what we created in our home but it's not important what they like or dislike about our home and our wardrobe; it is what we like. Do you truly care when you visit a family member or friends home if it is cluttered or dirty. You are only going to be there for a couple of hours. In the grand scheme of things what does it matter if they are messy or too tired to clean before you arrive.

I will never forget my Marine and I went to Florida for Christmas as a surprise visit to a close family member and we called this person to let them know we were ten minutes away. They said, oh no you can't come over until late this afternoon; we are not ready for you. We had to call another friend and visit them before we could go to our own family's home because they weren't ready. Ready for what, I wondered. We hadn't seen this family member for over a year yet they weren't ready for us. We don't care

> what their house looks like. We just wanted to
> visit them.

Hope you don't mind the tangents but this one above once tied into my mood swings because I would unconsciously care too much about what other people would think and I was a perfectionist. Now I don't care as much if my house isn't always immaculate or if my shirt has a tiny hole, when I run to the store. As long as I am not hurting anyone and I am practicing THE GOLDEN RULE and doing everything with love then I don't need to be concerned with the small stuff, do I?

Back to that really bad day, it wasn't just an off day that an ice cream cone could fix. It is one of those days that I not only struggle with being kind, considerate and sincere to others; it is when I am not kind, considerate and sincere to myself and GOD. These are days when I don't even like being around me. I wish I could sleep these days away and start fresh tomorrow. These days are the ones when you can feel yourself frowning for no reason. You look sick but feel physically fine. This is when nothing physically hurts but your mind is foggy. You don't have a head ache but just feel yucky. Have you ever had one of these days? If you haven't, you are blessed.

On my really bad days, which doesn't happen often anymore but they do sneak into my life periodically; I make an extra conscientious effort to be kind to myself and others who I come in contact with. As soon as I realize that this is going to be one of those days, I put on my heart pin or grab a hold of my blue heart stone in my car and ask GOD for extra strength for that day. These items will be available on line. HE then reminds me to take it slow, take care of Mary first, to let those close to me know that I am having a rough day, and ask for their patience. This way, if an uncomfortable situation arises, they know that it is me, not them, who is probably causing the dispute. It is easier for them to understand why I am grumpy. I continued to practice THE GOLDEN RULE as much as possible.

Especially when I think I might dip down to the mean Mary I used to be; I make sure I wear my heart pin. It's a cute pin that I can see when I go to the bathroom or walk past a mirror. It prompts me to do everything with love. I usually wear it when I am hurting and I know that the best way to handle the day is with love. Attached to my blouse, I hold it when I think I am about to do something mean and I know that I might not follow THE GOLDEN RULE. The heart pin gives me strength to turn the bad into good. It's sometimes magical. It really works for me. If I forget to wear my heart pin, I have a heart stone in my car that someone gave to me. In the heat of the moment I hold it. Holding these hearts creates my awareness that is necessary to get through whatever I am dealing with at the time. I wore it when I was struggling with some of the stories I shared above. I wore it daily when I was going through my divorce.

I didn't write on that really bad day. I should have because then I wouldn't have such a difficult time with this chapter. I know I was kind and considerate but not sincere. I had to force myself to be kind and considerate. Sincerity just wasn't available that day. My lips were turned down and to get them to face up was a struggle. A real smile was too hard to express. I found myself thinking about things that make me cry; things I know that I have no control over. Tears shed intermittently but no down pour. I like crying sometimes because I get it all out and can move on. That day I couldn't move on. I was stuck. So, I got done only what I absolutely had to, grabbed a couple of hugs throughout the day from my Marine and treated myself to a nice hot bath with soft music, candles and a glass of wine. While I was soaking in the tub; I gave myself credit and was actually proud that I handled the day with as much love as I could. It worked because when I went downstairs, I could actually feel the lifting of somberness. Not sure if it was the wine or getting later in the day and the tide was changing or just that I realized I did the best I could that day. It didn't matter, all I knew was I felt better. Knowing that I didn't hurt anyone because I was consciously aware that no matter how I felt I had to do everything with love.

I bet you don't even know how you are treating others on your bad days or your good days for some of you. You are probably so focused on all the junk and negativity in your life that you don't even think about who is tolerating your inconsiderate butt. Well, let me ask you, were you kind to those around you during your last mood swing? Should you apologize for your careless behavior?

It takes time to learn about ourselves and how we treat others. Some say it takes a life time. It sucks that it takes so long. We don't want it to take you so long. We want you to learn early in your life how to lead a happy, peaceful and content life so that you can Pay It Forward to those who aren't happy. Once you are able to help others, your life moves to another dimension. It is so successful. Getting there, maturing and growing with GOD'S LOVE is quite the journey. However, if you apply what We are teaching you, then you will be happier with more peace in your life. By practicing THE GOLDEN RULE and doing everything with love you will skip many unnecessary ugly experiences.

FORCE YOURSELF TO BE HAPPY
FAKE IT TILL YOU MAKE IT.

It might be hard to believe that being happy on a daily basis was an everyday challenge for me. Yep for years I had to train and diligently work on forcing a smile on my face. Some people have trouble with weight; I had trouble with staying happy. I'm blessed that I don't have problems with both at the same time. Watching my weight was actually easier for me than controlling my attitude. Now that I am happy, watching my weight is harder for me. It's finding the balance that will send me into nirvana. How about you, are you grumpy, cranky, grouchy, moody or are you blessed with being consistently happy?

Some days I was a really happy person; others I was a mess with a sad, cranky, grumpy or just unnecessarily snappy for no apparent reason. I didn't know how to create my own daily happiness until I reached out and searched for the meaning and secret to life. I would get upset, mad and down-right angry at the stupidest things almost daily. I wasted years of my life dancing with anger with the ones I loved the most. I knew I wasn't right but didn't know how to fix it. Does any of this sound familiar to you? On the days my loving spirit was not present I would search for it in the books that I read, tapes that I listened to, and friends that would be so kind to listen to me. Thank you Bill, Betty, Poppy, Kathy, Deb, Sue, Linda, Kenna, TJ and many others who loved me while I struggled through this journey of mine. I would journalize and questioned why I was grouchy more than I was happy. One of the reasons I was so unhappy was because I expected the men in my life to keep me fulfilled, laughing and excited.

It took me years to realize **I** controlled, created and maintained my happiness. For decades I intermittently sought help through counseling of all sorts. They kept taking me back to my childhood, blamed my parents, the men in my life and other events that occurred in my life. I got tired of blaming everyone and just wanted to fix me. GOD was not in my life at that time. I felt alone in my family of five. HE wasn't talking to me because I wasn't asking for HIS help. Sure I would talk to HIM when I was down and asked for HIS strength but We weren't communicating on a daily basis until the day HE hired me.

Let me explain. This is somewhat of a tangent but I thought you might want to know how I started working for GOD and maybe someday you could do the same. All you have to do is ask HIM how you can help and or repay HIM. I love telling this story; I appreciate you listening and I am also wondering if you have a similar one. If you do, please share it on my website. I will get back to forcing yourself to be happy in just a few minutes.

It was 2000, I was a single mom, working hard daily to raise my three sons. I was sitting at my desk, looking at my paycheck and I was please. Up early every morning, I had pounded the pavement five days a week in the heat and rain; going from business to business cold calling for eight hours a day to get this rewarding paycheck. That day I will never forget. I walked outside on my balcony; the sun was setting behind the majestic Koolau Mountain Range on the island of Oahu; the one on Hawaii Five O. I looked up into multi-colored sky with my hands raised high and thanked GOD for all the strength and wisdom HE had granted me to get my boys and I through what I had experienced that past year. Then I asked HIM how I could repay YOU. That is when HE answered me with HIS real voice. I WANT YOU TO SPREAD AS MUCH LOVE ON THIS EARTH AS YOU POSSIBLY CAN. IF YOU DO EVERYTHING WITH LOVE, YOU CANNOT FAIL. Wow, YOU spoke to me and told me what to do and how to do it. Whoa, I was in awe, shocked, a tad confused but yet honored that HE spoke to me.

I can do that I said. So I plop myself in front of my computer and start looking for men on love@aol.com, which was a free online dating website in 1999. That was the only love I comprehended at the time. I wasn't sure what HE want me to do so I did what I knew how to do. Shortly thereafter, my computer froze. I felt this tap on my shoulder and HE said, NOT WITH MEN, WITH WOMEN. I WANT YOU TO SPREAD AS MUCH LOVE AND HELP SINGLE WOMEN. That night I stayed up all night till 6am hand typing each email address and emailing over 300 women on this website in Hawaii telling them about my new single women's group. I don't know where I got the energy; it just came to me. The next day, I woke up in the afternoon to thirty or so emails and over a hundred women emailed me in a week. We were on to something. GOD knew they needed me. From there I started a Single

Women's Group in Hawaii and then again in
Orlando.

From that moment on, I did everything
I possibly could with love. My life changed
forever. I was on my way to a happier, more
peaceful, content life in this greedy, confused
and unloving world. My energy doubled, I was
on a mission for GOD. Eleven years later I am
still working for HIM with the same amount of
energy. HE rewards me immensely in so many
ways when I stay on HIS track. HE would do
the same for you.

Prior to that day though, I struggled with my divorce,
kids and everyday life situations; I was always on an
emotional rollercoaster. I expected my ex-husband and my
dates to create my happiness. Like I mentioned earlier, I
read and read many books about happiness but never found
one that convinced me that men don't create my happiness.
Many books said that I create my own happiness but none
changed my thought process.

While I was raising my children and attending to my
husband at the time, I searched for happiness through
books. My brother and friends took the time to listen to
why I was so unhappy and made many suggestions on how
I could lift my spirit. They all helped and the corroboration
of all my discoveries helped create who I am today.

During my identity crisis and in search for happiness,
I met another one of GOD'S Angels; a woman at an
AL-Anon meeting I attended. I am not sure who she was
or her name but her wisdom changed my life. AL-anon
is a wonderful organization which brings together family
and friends who are dealing with alcoholics in their life. As

you can see, I reached out for help in all directions. This is an example of doing my best. If you are on an emotional rollercoaster, are you reaching out for help? I hope so because this meeting changed my life forever. One of the attendees, GOD'S Angel, said something that puzzled me for days. She said, "Sometimes you have to force yourself to be happy and if you have to, fake it till you make it." Ok, that was interesting; I had to ponder this. I knew I could work with forcing myself to be happy but I am a real person and I don't like to fake anything. At that time, I wasn't ready to fake being happy. I just started to accept myself and see the truth for what it was. Now I thought to fake something would be going backwards. Nope. I wasn't willing to fake it till you make it just yet. For some reason though, my INNER VOICE kept repeating that sentence.

FORCE YOURSELF TO BE HAPPY AND IF YOU HAVE TO FAKE IT TILL YOU MAKE IT.

Always thinking of others, I decided to try it. My boys were young and they needed a happy mom. So as much as I possibly could at the time; I did force myself to be happy around them and my mean, at the time, alcoholic husband. Especially when I had my period; I was grumpy and emotional and everyone I was around reacted to my inconsiderate actions. If I couldn't force myself to be happy I would close my bedroom door and read about how I could make myself happy. It showed up again in my readings. Force yourself to be happy. Fake it till you make it. Thus, I knew I had to keep trying this method. I did and it worked for years. However, as I aged and became pre-menopausal I just couldn't force myself to be happy. I faked it so much that it hurt badly because at that time I was suppressing my true feelings and that is not what faking it till you make it means.

Faking it until you make it means that you force a smile on your face and think of something that makes you happy even when you are worried, grumpy, grouchy, irritable or angry at something you cannot change or is petty. Every situation is different. You have the choice of what is petty. As you mature, almost all of it is petty. We mostly want to address those who are unhappy for no apparent reason. The ones that are not naturally happy and there are a lot of us. Those who have a home and a decent life are the ones that need to fake a smile until it becomes real. It works, but you won't know until you try it. JUST TRY IT! Worry is a huge reason for unhappiness. If you are worried about how you are going to make it. Look around, do you have a roof over your head? Are you warm? Did you eat today? If you answered yes to these three questions and thanked GOD, you are surviving just fine, aren't you? It always works out. GOD will always provide if you have faith, especially if you have TOTAL FAITH. Now if you want more; go out and get more. If you want a mate, go find one. If you want a new car; take on a second job. First, ask yourself, what do you enjoy doing or why are you worried? This is a journey in itself. The sooner you get started the sooner you will be smiling. You do want to smile, don't you? It is up to you.

I had a family of five and an acre of beautiful land in Hawaii. The temperature was just right. My husband at the time, bless his generous heart, financially supported our family while I went to school and tended to the family needs. We took vacations with romantic evenings. Yet I still wasn't happy. I always wanted more. More love from him for my children. I was rarely satisfied, moody and didn't know how to appreciate all that he did do for us. It would have been great to have this golden book back then. I might have done a better job. However at the time, I didn't know any other way.

You see, I should have been happy but I wasn't. Sure junk was going on in my life but it wasn't only the ugly events that I created. I was unable to figure out a way to wake in the morning with a smile and keep it there. I held on to everyday issues and made them worst. Of course we had wonderful times in our family but I didn't know how to solve my problems with love and didn't have any guidelines like The 7 Golden Steps To Solve Your Negative Junk. That is why We are writing this golden book. GOD is tired of this greedy, confused and unloving world. I was never greedy but yes I was confused and unloving. So many of us are, are you?

Don't get me wrong, if you lost a family member or you are fighting a disease, or just broke up a marriage or relationship, by all means, grieve, be sad, angry or whatever emotion you need to express. Do not suppress these emotions. Go through The 7 Golden Steps To Solve Your Negative Junk and work on these issues with love. I am talking about when people are just grumpy, depressed, or worried because they can be and have really no reason to be in these rotten moods. The ones who complain about what they don't have and don't do anything to go get it. The ones who feel sorry for themselves when they have what they need and want more just to have more, are the ones We are telling to force themselves to be happy and fake it till you make it.

When my Marine and I were about to move to South Carolina; I was having pillow talk with one of my children. I was explaining that when we move we will be broke and won't be able to have much or share much with others. This young wise person said, "Why are you worried, you already have everything you need, don't you?" "What else do you need?" Wow, I needed a child to show me I have everything I need.

Subsequent to that bright, meaning the light bulb went off, pillow talk session, when I get unnecessarily worried about things that are probably not going to happen or are grumpy for no apparent reason. I stop, force myself to smile and take the time to thank GOD for the possessions I have already been granted and the job we have during this Great Recession that America is stressed with. It takes me just a few seconds to look around and thank GOD for my beautiful home, my animals, my Marine, my garden and everything else I can immediately think of. Instead of being worried about how I am going to make it; I realize I have made it. Dah.

I stopped thinking
start thanking
and just lived.

Then I listen to music, dance around my home and embraced how fortunate I am. I take an effort to find my Marine and thank him for working so hard and his smile rocks my world. I get busy doing an activity I enjoy; keeping a smile in my heart. It's not like I always have a permanent smile on face but I feel happier and at peace. I am content. Although the thought of walking around with a permanent smile sounds fun, it isn't realistic, at least right now it isn't. That is how I force myself to be happy and fake it till I make it. Keep busy and kick negative thoughts out of your head. Remember you can only have one thought at a time.

It sounds silly at first but it works for me and can work for you if you learn this clever process.

When I finally learned the golden skill to force myself to be happy and to fake it till I made it; I remained happier. I enjoy staying happy.

As my Marine tells me when I ask him why is he always so happy, he laughs. It's better than the alternative. He is so right.

I would like to share another quick story that goes along with creating your own happiness and being thankful for what we have. It was Christmas 2001. My Single Women's Group in Hawaii was growing. Christmas is a very difficult time for single women so I made sure I called as many as I could, to wish them a Merry Christmas. I ask what she was doing, not how she was doing because I didn't want the "fine" answer. She said she was singing Christmas carols and putting more ornaments on the tree. She was baking a pie and fixing a nice Christmas dinner for herself and thanking GOD she was able to do so. Now I knew she was alone because we talked earlier in the week. She has no family on the island. I was so proud of her that I cannot stop telling her story. She told me nobody is going to create her Christmas for her so she will have to make it happen herself. Make it happen herself is exactly what she did. She was so grateful that she could afford the beautiful tree and the pretty ornaments that went on her tree. WOW!! Why didn't I think of that when I was alone. She too was one of GOD'S Angel lent to me. Here I thought I was her angel by calling her on my busy Christmas day but she was mine. Ever since that day; I make a huge effort to make every one of my days, especially holidays special because no one is going to do it exactly the way I want it. She was in my life for a reason and only a season.

Presently, my being and staying happy is almost natural. I finally do it daily. I don't have to force myself to put a smile on my face and in my heart because it is already there. I actually had to teach myself it is more fun to smile than it is to frown. Those of you who are naturally happy my hat goes off to you. My Marine doesn't create my happiness but he does get credit for contributing to my being happy because he is 99% of the time happy. It is easier to be happy when you surround yourself with happy people. Thank you sweetheart!

Being Happy is
better than the alternative

Most days, I create each day exactly the way I want it. If I do have tough days and I can't over-come being grouchy and unloving; I first make sure I cannot get out of my funk and accept it; then embrace it. That's when I listen, read or watch something funny. I record all of Ellen Degenerates shows especially for those days I am having difficulty smiling. These are Mary days. I need this time to recharge my batteries. Often times, I find that I cannot function well on these days and that is ok.

These bad days are actually necessary to appreciate the good ones. This has to do with the balance of life; which I discuss in my next book, Be The Better Partner. For now, take time to learn about yourself. Search for activities that you feel good participating in. Do your homework on you. Turn the television off and get to work on you until you are smiling more than you are blah. Get up an hour earlier and read or listen to good spiritual books. It took me until 45 years to really get to know, love myself, and find happiness, peace, and to be content in this greedy, confused, unloving world.

To Summarize:

- Analyze your bad days
- Mean People SUCK
- Are you a mean and moody? Do you need to work on you? Are you the cause of your unhappiness
- A loving spirit is the same attitude you had when you were dating. Do you have an example of your loving spirit? Please share it with me on our website.
- Mood swings are a teaching mechanism that will help you balance your inner self. You will soon be able to appreciate them.
- Mood swings are a form of a temporary mental illness that can be healed just like a physical wound.
- Having abnormalities is normal. What abnormalities do you have? Which do you need to work on changing? Which ones should you accept and embrace? Remember the Serenity Prayer
- Be proud that you are different!
- Has any of these concepts clicked yet?
- What are your qualities?
- DON'T GOSSIP OR JUGDE. Feel empathy for those that do.
- Mental pain is just as painful as physical pain.
- Go to hiddenwounds.org and donate whatever you can please.
- If you have to talk, compliment that person you are about to say something bad about. Look for one good thing about them. Or walk away, repeating, I will do everything with love, I will do everything

with love. Be extremely kind and don't give them a single reason to treat you with disrespect.

- FOR GOD'S SAKE, JUST BE THE BETTER PERSON!
- If you are mean, unnecessarily angry, or unkind, you are mentally ill. Admit it and work on fixing you. Don't keep walking down the same street
- Don't be embarrassed if you have to take a pill temporarily to help you battle your mood swings. Talk and if you should, apologize to your loved ones. Let them know you are on a mission.
- In the grand scheme of things, what does it really matter?
- Heart pins and other items are online to remind you on a daily basis to do everything with love.
- FORCE YOURSELF TO BE HAPPY
- FAKE IT TILL YOU MAKE IT.
- My story how GOD asked me to work for HIM. HE will tell how you can serve HIM if you ask.
- Be on the look out for GOD'S Angels. They are all around you. Please tell me your story when HE lent one to you.
- Make every day and especially holidays special because no one is going to make them happen for you.
- Being happy is better than the alternative, isn't it?

CHAPTER 7

PAY IT FORWARD

Have you ever seen the movie *Pay It Forward*? If not, rent it or buy it and watch it with anyone you love. Better yet, watch it with someone you are angry with. What a concept this book and movie has to offer. The author of *Pay It Forward* is Catherine Ryan Hyde, who is definitely one of GOD'S Angels.

Pay It Forward is about a boy, Trevor, who is given an assignment by his Social Studies teacher. Their assignment is to come up with an idea that would make this world a better place. Well, he comes up with a remarkable concept; it is called Pay it Forward. Pay It Forward is when one person does something good for three people without expecting anything in return. Once those three people get helped or are given something then those three people help, give, or do something to benefit three other people and it continues to branch down like building a pyramid from the top down. Please watch the movie and visit the website payitforward. com; it is an amazing idea. I always wondered why that movie meant so much to me. Many years ago, an acquaintance actually gave me the poster board from the movie. Now why in the world would he go through all that trouble to make sure I got it? It is because GOD wanted me to see it every day to remind me I have work to do for HIM. Simply amazing!

Well, most of us cannot give a jaguar away, or bring a homeless man into our home. Also, it would be an extreme stretch for each of us to help three people who help three people. I don't want to spoil the movie so I don't need to tell you anymore. However, we are utterly capable to deliver one sincere compliment to just one other human every day, aren't we? GOD is giving everyone who wants it, an extra credit assignment. HE wants us to give at least one sincere compliment to someone every day. Let's just say:

A COMPLIMENT A DAY
KEEPS MADNESS AWAY

HE also wants us to compliment and/or show our appreciation to those we live with, at least once a week. It would be wonderful to do it more than once a day but for most people, unfortunately, that might be asking too much. So We want to keep it simple. A compliment a day is simple. For those of us who are bless with the ability to effortlessly compliment others sincerely, we are assigned by GOD to give more than one a day and to reach out to complete strangers as often as the opportunity arises. You know who you are; most likely you are already doing so. HE knows it and very much appreciates you for doing so.

If every one of us on this earth would sincerely say one kind compliment to one person every day, our world would be a better place to live, don't you agree?

GOD agrees.

What if we were taught when we were young that complimenting someone is just as important as saying please or thank you? If all the parents of the world took the time to make sure they give a compliment a day to their children and that each family member give a compliment a day to someone; people would feel more appreciated and loved and this world would be a much better place. Of course teenagers might rebel of this idea at first. Often times it is a challenge for the parent to find something nice to say about their juveniles. However if the parents would step up, be The Better Person and do their best to consistently reminded their children with love, it will inevitably be instilled in their head. Thus, when they have children, they will most likely teach them to give a compliment a day. Again, this is not just a book, it is a campaign. We want you to help Us change the world. If there is a will there is a way. It is just a choice. You will be rewarded because you will be happier, more peaceful and content in this greedy, confused, unloving world and so will those around you.

Just curious, when was the last time you received a sincere compliment? How did it feel when you were recognized? Everyone enjoys compliments, don't they? If you say you don't then you are just not right. We don't enjoy false compliments. However we do take pleasure in any variety of sincere praise, admiration, approval, accolades, commendation, tributes, kudos, comments, acknowledgement, awards, flatter and/or encomium (I didn't even know what that meant), but it is a synonym.

Appreciation is a typical human craving. Many won't admit that it is important to be noticed and some will say that we are considered insecure if we need approval from others. This just out, we are all insecure in some way or another; aren't we Dr. Phil, Oprah and Ellen? As wonderful as they are, yet they too are not perfect. Not one of us is perfect enough to say that we are totally, I mean, completely secure with who we are and, everything we say and do. My point here is not to talk about security but to express that every one of us needs to be loved and appreciated, for us to grow into healthy loving humans.

If you look around the people that are loved and appreciated are successful in so many ways. Many that aren't appreciated and loved are in prison. By the way, success doesn't necessarily mean money. Success to me is being happy, peaceful and content. Many say that they don't need to be appreciated and it is probably because someone is/ has appreciated them through unobvious compliments. Sure we shouldn't need approval from others because we are supposed to find happiness within ourselves and create our own happiness but isn't it nice when someone tells you that you did a great job or that you are glowing with GOD'S LOVE. That's a huge compliment. I mentioned earlier that I can tell those who love GOD with all their heart because they glow and have a dolphin smile when I meet them. I tell them so. I compliment people sincerely almost every day I go out of my house. If I don't leave my property, I compliment my Marine, my dog and my new kitten. I know that sounds ridiculous to some but even they need to hear how wonderful they are. My dog is the best dog in the whole wide world. My compliments to them are sincere as well.

This I must admit, I am blessed in this area. This golden skill is the next level in becoming The Better Person. Since I have worked so hard at doing everything with love, GOD has blessed me with the golden skill to look for something that I like about what they are wearing, or one feature, their hair, face, body, clothing, accessories, shoes, child, and especially if they have a nice smile. With men I am cautious and have many times said, I hope you don't mind and I am not flirting with you but I would like to share with you that you have very pretty eyes or lashes or something that is easy on the eyes. The reaction is a blush, with a smile.

Their smile is my reward.

Even if I don't like all 65 body piercings or tattoos all over their body; I compliment them on their creativity. It is sincere, I won't ever get piercings or tatoos like they have but I like it because it is what makes them different and kudos for them for their individuality. I take effort to make another human's day a little brighter by verbalizing it to them. I do it because I know it makes them feel good. I gave them a reason to smile. GOD told me my job on this earth to share as much love as I possibly can and this is how I do it. I don't judge them. Making them feel good makes me feel great. So I take a few seconds to look for something on them or about them to mention so that they can smile too. HE wants you to do the same. Can you compliment someone every day or are you so self-righteous, that you don't have the time. I surely hope not. This is a message from GOD folks, not me. I didn't think of this. I don't get credit for this. I am just the messenger.

Even if only a million of us followed through with GOD'S extra credit assignment; our world would be a much nicer place. We can make a difference. With this extra credit assignment we could start a revolution. A loving revolution that generates a smile, not a war revolution that causes tears, is what We want to initiate. We want parents to consistently acknowledge their children of their accomplishments and so they too will contagiously complement those around them. The more you do it, the more it will get done by others. Children learn from example; if they hear us, as parents, complimenting each other they will follow suit. Of course, again, we don't need to be the polite gophers in Chapter 4. Life is a balance. If we would do it just a little more often that would suffice. There is no need to go from one extreme to the other.

Instead of asking people, "how are you?" I tell them I hope they are having a good day. Why do people ask how they are doing when they don't really care? To be polite or is it because they just don't know what to say. I don't know why I feel this way but I think it is insincere, a waste of time, and inconsiderate to ask how are you if you really don't want to know. How about changing, how are you to either just a hello, I like your smile or I hope you are having a good day or again, just hi. I stopped saying how are you when I heard about the following incident. A young woman in an office greeted everyone in the morning. It went like this:

Young woman said, "Good morning how are you?"
Office co-worker answered the rhetorical question, "Fine thank you."
Young woman responded, "Good, I am really glad to hear that."

For months the same morning greeting:
Young woman said, "Good morning how are you?"
Office co-worker answered the rhetorical question, "Fine thank you."
Young woman responded, "Good, I am really glad to hear that."

This went on for months. Until the conversation, if you want to call it that, went like this:
Young woman said, "Good morning how are you?"

Office co-worker answered the question, "My dog died."

Young woman not really listening or caring, responded, "Good, I am really glad to hear that." She went on about her work and the co-worker and office associates couldn't believe it.

It became such an insincere routine that it became hurtful. My Marine says it is the way people are brought up to politely acknowledge their presence and often times helps start the conversation. To me it is living in fear. If you were living in love then there is no need to say anything but hello, I hope you are having a nice day, or just a smile. Lately when someone ask me how are you, I reply, I am blessed thank you. I don't ask them how they are because I don't normally have the time to listen to the real answer. It's hard to change a habit when it's been around for so long.

When was the last time you sincerely complimented your partner? Do you find yourself gossiping about the people in your life more often or do you have admiring comments and praise for them more often? Why do you think is it so much easier for you to talk negatively about people than it is to compliment them? Please take a moment to answer. Please write your answers on my website: bethebetterperson.org.

Do you know that GOD would be extremely pleased if you praised the ones you love the same as you praise HIM. HE told me HE doesn't need to be worshipped. HE would rather have you spend less time worshiping HIM and more time practicing THE GOLDEN RULE and doing more with love. If everyone in the world lived by THE GOLDEN RULE, do unto others as you would want them to do unto you, and everyone really tried to do everything with love, we would have world peace.

A great place to start is with a compliment a day. GOD loves compliments too. When I tell HIM what a great job HE did on the sunrise or sunset this morning, I can feel HIM shining on me even when the sun isn't up. Or when one of my flowers bloom, I ask if that is Mother Nature or HIM. We joke about it because really they are the same. Call me crazy, but call me happy, peaceful and full of love.

You know how sometimes we get up on the wrong side of the bed and have a bad day at work and want to come home and kick the dog. We know that is just a saying; I would never hurt an animal but sometimes we feel that way because not one person said anything that gave us a reason to smile and stand proud. Most of the time people demand so much from us and don't realize if they just said a few sincere complimenting words; we would probably work harder. I know when my old boss Mark would tell me what a great job I was doing and that he had never seen anyone as friendly as me; I would stay out selling an extra hour just for him. It really does work for most people. A compliment a day could turn someone's day around. Wouldn't you like to give people a reason to smile?

Maybe you are not ready to Pay It Forward with a compliment a day and that is ok too. You must be hurting. Fix you first. However for those of you who have enjoyed what We have shared with you and are feeling some of the results of practicing THE GOLDEN RULE throughout your day and are doing everything with love then go ahead, take it to the next level and try to verbalize a compliment a day to one person or more. You can never give too many compliments out; unless, of course, they are insincere. The feeling is GREAT! It also shows GOD that you really do love HIM and want to work for HIM.

Also, let me tell you a secret you probably already know.

THE MORE YOU GIVE, THE MORE YOU GET

I'm a giver. I love giving compliments, presents, money, my time or anything I am capable. I know many people are not like me when it comes to giving and that's a good thing. Sometimes I give way more than I should but it is funny how I always have and receive everything I need and many extra wants. I do not feel complete unless I am giving. Sharing with others, even when I didn't have much to share made me happy and if you are not happy and in search of fulfillment then try giving more. It will not only come back to you two to three times more when you need it the most but the feeling of knowing that you helped someone is so enlightening.

A couple of months ago, I needed a tax write off and I remember that the gifts I gave at Christmas were tax deductible. I stopped in the community center and although I was there to get something for myself, I ended up writing a check to help a single mom for her heat bill. I had planned to spend that money on my new furniture for our new lanai but I pictured myself with my three boys without heat and I gladly wrote her a check and my new furniture had to wait for my next pay day. While I was writing the check my INNER VOICE advised me to write it for the full amount she needed instead of just the month she was late. I hesitated because I was thinking selfishly about my new furniture. However, it was GOD who told me to do so and I smiled and laughed a little because I knew I was talking to GOD and at that moment I saw that the director of the center shed a tear. WOW!!!! My furniture can wait; no problem. There was such joy in the room. She did thank me over and over. I just told her to have the single mom Pay It Forward. Well, I sold, sold and sold the entire month. I won a contest and I had one of my best months ever and a big check to buy top quality furniture. We are telling you, the more you give the more you will receive.

I also like to give randomly. I think it is so much fun to pay for the car behind me when I am at a drive through at a fast food restaurant or pay for someone's parking when you know it is going to be the same as mine. I don't go over-board, I don't think. I just know that the more I give the more I will get. However, I don't think of the getting when I am donating. Yet, I do imagine the person's face when they receive the gift even if I am not present to hand it to them. When I paid for the single mother's heat, I didn't get to meet her but I knew that night her and her kids were going to be warm. When I am watching television in the evening, I think about how I made their life a little more comfortable and I hope that they will Pay It Forward.

If you have a job, please give at least 10% of your income or volunteer your time to someone or some organization. Give more than just to your church. Or give some to your church and then find an organization that you would like to get involved with. Instead of building up your church with fine décor; give to other organizations like Hidden Wounds, animal shelters, feeding sheltering and educating America, or some other organization where you can make a difference. Giving to your church is fine but I get so disappointed when the owner of the church wants more money to buy more things to make the church bigger and fancier. When it does get bigger and filled with ornate material things, it is still not good enough. GOD doesn't care what HIS house looks like. HE does care about spreading as much love as we can. That is why HE asked me to write this golden book. One of the churches in our town actually tried to sell their CD for their own personal income. Many of them talk constantly about tithing in their sermon. I say shame on them. It's good that you support your church but people need help right now and we need to help people not build bigger and more ornate churches. I get so turned off when churches do this. Build a church with practicing THE GOLDEN RULE and teach every one of its members to do everything with love and that is when the money will come pouring in. Again, don't get me wrong, it's good to give to your church but if your church is buying unnecessary lavish decor; I ask you to take a look at what is really necessary in a church.

Also, if you cannot donate monetarily then surely you can make time to volunteer for someone who needs your help. Please don't just only volunteer your time at Thanksgiving or Christmas, help is needed all year round in so many organizations. I played BINGO with our elderly Veterans. I know that some way, somehow they contributed to my freedom. The least I can do is visit them and share a smile. There are so many, many things you can volunteer your time. Just a couple of hours a week will be so fulfilling and GOD will reward you for your efforts. Remember, it's not all about you. I have many hobbies that I would rather be doing but when I take the time to get out and volunteer my time so that someone else could smile; it is so much better than a selfish hobby. However, you will have to take the first step and try it. Again, help make a difference and get off the computer, stop wasting time tweeting, turn off the television unless you are watching the movie Pay It Forward, and Pay It Forward. Help Us spread this golden book around to those who need it.

To Summarize:

- Please watch, rent or buy the movie: *Pay It Forward*
- GOD'S extra credit assignment:
- A COMPLIMENT A DAY KEEPS THE MADNESS AWAY
- We are utterly capable to deliver one sincere compliment a day.
- **If every one of us on this earth would sincerely say one kind compliment to one person every day, our world would be a better place to live, don't you agree?**
- Parents please teach your children to sincerely compliment one person a day; share at the dinner table how this was accomplished
- We do take pleasure in any variety of sincere praise, admiration, approval, accolades, commendation, tributes, kudos, comments, acknowledgement, awards, flatter and/or encomium, don't we?
- Look for something; make an effort to compliment someone every day. Just one
- Instead of asking people "how are you?" Just say hello and find something about them that is cute, nice, beautiful, or tell them I hope you are having a good day.
- Tell me about your Pay It Forward compliment
- Spend less time worshiping GOD and more time practicing THE GOLDEN RULE
- THE MORE YOU GIVE THE MORE YOU GET but don't think about the getting part.

- Give to more than your church. Spread your tithings to those in need not on building a fancier church.
- Volunteer. Eventually there will be a list on my website.
- Get out of the house and go help someone, anyone!

CONCLUSION

LIVE THIS GOLDEN BOOK

Yesterday I had another remarkable moment with GOD. Unbelievable, even for me but I truly do believe because it actually did happened to me. My Marine is also blown away.

As I was driving yesterday after what we call a no sale I was a little disappointed because I knew I could have done a better job but didn't have the patience. I was doing almost everything with love but when someone starts to boss you around and say, I am about to ask you to leave; it is not that easy. Like I have mentioned before; I have not mastered these golden skills.

So my drive home was low-spirited. I am also feeling bitter because I had to drive over 150 miles and my manager, who is also my husband, assigned another loan officer the appointment I wanted which is closer to our home. He felt he had to give her the closer appointment because we are about to lose this loan officer. She too is driving long distances and working every day. This job is hard on my body. My hip hurts when I drive these long distances and that is the only reason I want a closer appointment.

We are required to call our manager after every sales call. I called him. I spoke to him in a crabby and short tone. I took my no sale out on him when I shouldn't have. I got off the phone knowing that I shouldn't have spoken to him that way and GOD spoke to me. "YOU NEED TO LIVE OUR GOLDEN BOOK. GO HOME KISS YOUR MARINE HELLO, JUST LIKE YOU SAY YOU DO IN OUR GOLDEN BOOK. DON'T BE A HIPPOCRITE. YOU NEED TO LIVE IT TOO, NOT JUST WRITE IT. YOU MUST PRACTICE WHAT WE ARE PREACHING. I WILL MAKE YOU A DEAL. GO HOME AND THE MOMENT YOU WALK IN THE DOOR DROP YOUR STUFF AND GO KISS HIM HELLO AND I WILL TAKE THE PAIN IN YOUR HIP AWAY."

I am a pretty stubborn person sometimes. I must admit I don't like that I am bossy and want things my way. I was sore and I knew that if I did what GOD asked me to do I would be relieved from pain. So I did exactly that and guess what happened. YEP. A few seconds after I kissed my hubby; I even hugged him, my pain was gone. POOF. Yes, magic. I write this morning and I have had not one ounce of pain all morning and all last night. Freaking amazing!!!! I told my Marine and I think he believes but not really sure. It doesn't matter if he does believe because all this happens to me not him. Frankly, I don't care who believes me. All I know is GOD wants me to live Our golden book so I can be proud and teach others.

This morning as I write; it just so happens I was working on the Conclusion of this golden book and I wasn't sure how to go about it. Now I know, all I need to say is

LIVE THIS GOLDEN BOOK

because it is the secret to your happy, peaceful, content life in this greedy, confused unloving world.

I just asked GOD if HE would like to have the last word and HE said, "THANK YOU MARY"

You are so welcome. I love you! Please give me the love, wisdom, time, and whatever else it might take to share this golden book with others so WE (that is you, as well) can make OUR world a better place.

TO SUMMERIZE

- **FOR GOD'S SAKE, BE THE BETTER PERSON!**

APPENDIX

BOOKS TO READ

Conversations with GOD: Book 1
     By: Neale Donald Walsch

Dance With Anger
     By: Dr. Harriet Lerner

Feel The Fear And Do It Anyway
     By: Susan Jeffers, Ph.D.

Choosing Happiness
     By: Veronica Ray

In The Meantime
     By Iyanla Vanzant

Power For Living
     By: Jamie Buckingham

Courage to Change
     By: AL-Anon Family Groups

How To Win Friends & Influence People
     By: Dale Carnegie

Love
By: Leo Buscaglia

Don't Sweat The Small Stuff
By: Richard Carlson

Mary Kay
By: Mary Kay

The Total Money Makeover
By: Dave Ramsey

The 7 Habits of Highly Effective People
By: Stephen R. Covey

Life Strategies
By: Phillip C. McGraw

How To Stop Worrying and Start Living
By: Dale Carnegie

Your Erroneous Zones
By: Dr. Wayne Dyer